Praise for the First Edition

"[Keenan's books] read like very good sermons or college lectures by a priest both learned and engaged in the world. By making the Catholic tradition come alive, the books invite moral reflection and struggle."—*Theological Studies*

"A readable, uncommonly good book that should be required reading for anyone preparing for or engaged in pastoral ministry."—*Library Journal*

"This is a lovely book! Keenan probes his own experiences of struggle, suffering and love, interweaving them with biblical reflection and theological analysis. He looks fault and sorrow squarely in the face, yet sustains buoyant notes of hope and commitment. The content of this book is an exercise in the virtue of its title."—Lisa Sowle Cahill, J. Donald Monan Professor of Theology, Boston College

"Imagine a book that is at once a source of profound wisdom, a systematic presentation of a moral and ethical tradition, and a 'page-turner'! This is what James Keenan's *Moral Wisdom* turns out to be. There is nothing facile about this volume, nothing superficial, nothing manipulative. It weaves together autobiography, the stories of others, interpretation of biblical and theological texts, and a deep understanding of what morality is and what the Roman Catholic tradition of moral theology has been and can be when it is at its best. Few will come away from reading this book without imaginative new hope, salutary appreciation for 'hard sayings,' new insight into the meaning of divine mercy, and perhaps experiences of both laughter and the 'gift of tears.' Thought-provoking and informative, opening questions and not shutting them down: here is a significant contribution to ongoing explorations of the moral life."—Margaret A. Farley, Gilbert Stark Professor of Christian Ethics, Yale University Divinity School

"Father Jim Keenan is one of today's foremost moral theologians. *Moral Wisdom* reflects his distinctive combination of intellectual mastery of the tradition and sensitivity to today's concerns. He places the older, 'sin-oriented' approach to moral theology within its proper context in a sapiential tradition of moral reflection, in a way that is at one and the same time intellectually satisfying and pastorally accessible. While this book is intended predominantly for a general audience, it is also rich in insights for professionals in the field. I recommend it highly and look forward to its publication."—Jean Porter, John A. O'Brien Professor of Theology at the University of Notre Dame, author of *Natural and Divine Law: Reclaiming the Tradition for Christian Ethics*

"Father James Keenan is one of those rare contemporary theologians who compellingly weave together rich pastoral experience and masterful intellectual inquiry. To read him is to hear not only the considered wisdom of Catholic moral teaching, but to have the privilege of hearing a learned man struggling to work out his own moral practices. In this book, lay readers and scholars alike can see how Catholic moral tradition informs a life of discernment, love, and everyday courage."—Tom Beaudoin, Fordham University, author of *Consuming Faith*

"James Keenan puts 'flesh and bones' on the abstractions of moral theory and demonstrates from his own personal experience how the Christian moral life is a pilgrimage of faith, hope and love. Keenan's book will be used widely in college classrooms and seminaries alike. His clarity, honesty and passion ought to be emulated by every moral theologian."—Stephen J. Pope, Boston College

MORAL WISDOM

LESSONS AND TEXTS FROM THE CATHOLIC TRADITION

Second Edition

JAMES F. KEENAN, S.J.

A Sheed & Ward Book
an imprint of
ROWMAN & LITTLEFIELD PUBLISHERS, INC.
Lanham • Boulder • New York • Toronto • Plymouth, UK

A SHEED & WARD BOOK

Published by Rowman & Littlefield Publishers, Inc.
A wholly owned subsidiary of The Rowman & Littlefield Publishing Group, Inc.
4501 Forbes Boulevard, Suite 200, Lanham, Maryland 20706
http://www.rowmanlittlefield.com

Estover Road, Plymouth PL6 7PY, United Kingdom

British Library Cataloguing in Publication Information Available

Library of Congress Cataloging-in-Publication Data
Keenan, James F.
  Moral wisdom : lessons and texts from the Catholic tradition / James F. Keenan. —
2nd ed.
     p. cm.
  Includes bibliographical references and index.
  ISBN 978-1-4422-0296-2 (cloth : alk. paper) — ISBN 978-1-4422-0297-9 (pbk. : alk.
paper) — ISBN 978-1-4422-0298-6 (electronic)
  1. Christian ethics—Catholic authors. I. Title.
  BJ1249.K377 2010
  241'.042—dc22   2009032415

The paper used in this publication meets the minimum requirements of American
National Standard for Information Sciences—Permanence of Paper for Printed Library
Materials, ANSI/NISO Z39.48-1992.

Printed in the United States of America

To Deb
with love

CONTENTS

Part II: The Texts

Part III: The Future

PREFACE

In 1953 I was born in Brooklyn. I was raised there until I was thirteen, when, after the birth of my sister, Jeannine, Mom and Dad decided that our family of seven needed another bedroom. We moved out to Smithtown, Long Island.

Growing up in Brooklyn was remarkable. My dad was a police officer, first working in Williamsburg, then in the youth squad, until finally he arrived in Manhattan South Homicide. My mom was a homemaker, and besides raising the five of us, she was also a typist.

Living in Brooklyn, or more specifically, St. Thomas Aquinas's parish on Flatbush and Flatlands Avenue, we eventually became, like everyone else, involved in the parish. Mom was in the Rosary Altar Society, Dad in Holy Name, and I was an altar boy. With my brothers and sisters, we attended the parish grammar school. The girls were taught by the Sisters of Mercy, the boys by lay teachers in the lower grades and by the Brothers of the Holy Cross in the upper grades. The two schools were packed. There were two classes for each grade in each school and a class could range anywhere between fifty-five and seventy-five students. I don't know how the teachers did it.

In that environment I learned about the fullness of the church and its traditions. For instance, on All Saints, we traipsed to school dressed like the saint after whom we were named. I had my white robes, white beard, and my walking staff, my friend Peter dragged a big set of keys, and my brother, Bobby—well, my mom was convinced that the eleventh-century abbot was bald. In that school, we learned about saints, prayers, the commandments, the corporal works of mercy, the sacraments, the life of Jesus, and so on. Each of us had enough theological language at the age of ten that our teachers were proud of us.

In a variety of ways we shared a moral wisdom. What Bobby and I learned in school, or what my parents learned in their associations both in the church and among their friends, was a type of moral wisdom. We—you and I—were taught through a variety of venues and methods to know which values to pursue and which virtues to embody. Sermons and pageants about the pilgrim, the martyr, and the abbot along with their vigilance, courage, and fidelity taught us not only about who we were, but also about who we could become.

That moral wisdom is and always has been available. Our tradition is a lively, life-giving one, even though some use the term *tradition* to halt reflection, discussion, education, insight, wisdom, development, or growth. In its richer meaning, however, tradition is always progressive, developing, and constantly calling us to receive it, enrich it, and humanize it. Entering into that tradition as a community is what I want to do with this book on *Moral Wisdom*.

ACKNOWLEDGMENTS

THE SUBJECT MATTER OF THE "LESSONS" AND "TEXTS" WAS FIRST given as a series of eight lectures at St. Ignatius Loyola Parish, New York City, under the auspices of the pastor, the Reverend Walter Modrys, S.J. Subsequently, I presented the lessons as a series of lectures at the Loyola School of Theology at the Ateneo de Manila in Quezon City, the Philippines, under the sponsorship of the president, the Reverend Victor Salonga, S.J., with the kind assistance of Dr. Patria Arañaz. "Hope and Leadership" was a keynote address to a leadership conference chaired by Mr. Francis Butler and sponsored by FADICA (Foundations and Donors Interested in Catholic Activities, Inc.). I am grateful to all these people for making these events engaging, hospitable, and life-enhancing.

I rewrote my lectures while at the Loyola House of Studies in Quezon City. I experienced great consolation there mostly due to the Jesuit community's hospitality and above all the scholastics' extraordinary generosity. Many friends in Manila also made my summer's work easy by their engaging companionship, and I want to name five of them: Luis David, Karen Enriquez, Ritchie Genilo, Lúcás Chan Yiu Sing, and Jordy Orbe.

I want to thank all those at Sheed & Ward, especially my editor, Mr. Jeremy Langford, for their adept and talented work in publishing this project.

Finally, I dedicate this book to my sister, Deb. Her life has an integrity, a depth, and a complexity that routinely awakens my rather ordinary life. She touches my life with a grace that has been with me now for many, many years. To her, her husband Gary, and their son Jon, and, of course, Megan, with love and gratitude.

NEW EDITION

Last year Ross Miller and then Sarah Stanton at Rowman and Little-field encouraged me to do a new edition of this book. They canvassed a number of authors and sent me a new set of reviewers' comments that helped me fashion, I think, a better book. T.I. made quite a number of changes.

Whenever I refer to a scriptural text, I now present a summary of the passage. To each of the nine chapters I append questions so as to get you, the reader, more directly engaged.

Every chapter has been edited. For instance, in chapter 3 I developed lengthy reflections on social sin, and in chapter 7 I added a discussion comparing mercy and justice. Three chapters were basically overhauled. Chapter 2 on "Conscience" is now much more focused. Chapter 4 on "Suffering" is completely reorganized. Chapter 5 on Jesus and the Gospels was completely rewritten, assuming more classical concerns on the Jesus of history and the Christ of faith. I think now *Moral Wisdom* is clearer, more comprehensive, and more contemporary, while still very much rooted in the tradition.

This then is a new edition responding to its last five years of use. I want to thank both Ross and Sarah, as well as the three anonymous reviewers who gave me much to think about and much to do.

Moral Wisdom beyond the Moral Manuals

T HE MOST RECENT SUSTAINED HISTORICAL STUDY OF MORAL theology was delivered through a series of eight lectures at Oxford University fifteen years ago by John Mahoney, S.J. The work was titled *The Making of Moral Theology*.[1] Recently, Oxford University Press commissioned two American Christian ethicists to bring twenty-five colleagues together to write on different topics relevant to the field of Christian ethics, especially over the past one hundred years.[2] Among the twenty-five essays that they assigned, five deal with contemporary classics, and Mahoney's book is one of them. In his book, Mahoney argues that the source of the discipline of moral theology is the Irish penitentials of the fifth and sixth centuries. A brief look at these penitentials will help us build a better understanding of the foundation and evolution of moral theology and its application in people's everyday lives.

The Texts of Moral Theology: The Penitentials, the Confessional Manuals, and the Moral Manuals

For many centuries monks carried with them little books of guidelines for administering a fair penance to their spiritual "directees" who sought on occasion forgiveness of their sins. These "penitentials" were later developed from the seventh to the twelfth century by other abbots throughout Britain and continental Europe. They were, in all likelihood, the only written texts that specifically dealt with morality at that time.[3]

In the early thirteenth century, Pope Innocent III, a fascinating figure who was the first to cast off the title of "Vicar of Peter" in order to assume his newly minted title "Vicar of Christ" (an enormous shift!), imposed upon the entire church the Easter duty. For the first time every Christian was required to receive communion once a year at Easter, but in order to do that, they had to confess her or his sinfulness to a priest. Henry Lea, the great Protestant church historian, called this the most significant piece of legislation in the history of the church.[4]

Innocent's edict prompted the need for training priests as confessors. In 1221 he turned to the newly founded Order of Preachers (the Dominicans) and told them that they were to have as their mission the hearing of confessions. As a result, the Dominicans, an order whose charism was originally to preach the Gospel, was dramatically changed. To meet the papal charge almost all Dominicans were required to attend daily the lectures about confessional practice.[5] The theological formation of the Dominican orders became, for the most part, instruction on hearing confessions. A series of textbooks called "the summaries of confessional manuals," the sequel to the penitentials' "sequel," appeared from the thirteenth to the sixteenth centuries.

In the sixteenth century, with expansionism into the New World and the Far East, European moralists reexamined what was sin and what was not, especially with regard to the exercises of power and money, and particularly, in the latter case, lending practices, investments, and maritime insurance issues. In rethinking their moral teachings (always in the key of what was sin and what was not), they speculated a great deal and reorganized the way we think morally. After a century of innovation, moralists settled down and distilled their judgments into textbooks, which were first known as "summaries of cases" and then as "moral manuals." These textbooks lasted until the Second Vatican Council (1962–1965).

Like the "penitentials" and the "confessional manuals," these "moral manuals" were all about sin. They were only for confessors. They were specifically differentiated from any type of devotional literature that helped lay and religious persons grow in the states of perfection or, as we would say today, into being better disciples.

By the seventeenth century, moral theologians were so convinced that the task of moral theology was *solely* to teach the priest how to determine in confession what was sin (and what was its due penance) that they effectively cut the first principle of the natural law in half. That first principle is simple: avoid evil and do good. Morals were about avoiding evil; devotional literature was about doing the good.

At the beginning of the twentieth century these manuals of moral theology began to appear in the vernacular, though the material that pertained to the sixth commandment remained in Latin so as not to be an occasion of sin for the untrained reader. In order to appreciate just how the self-understanding of the moral theologian focused singularly on the confessional, we can look at the preface of the first manual of moral theology in English, which was written by an English Jesuit, Thomas Slater:

> [Moral theology] is the product of centuries of labor bestowed by able and holy men on the practical problems of Christian ethics. Here, however, we must ask the reader to bear in mind that the manuals of moral theology are technical works intended to help the confessor and the parish priest in the discharge of their duties. They are as technical as the text-books of the lawyer and the doctor. They are not intended for edification, nor do they hold up a high ideal of Christian perfection for the imitation of the faithful. They deal with what is of obligation under pain of sin; they are books of moral pathology. They are necessary for

the Catholic priest to enable him to administer the sacrament of Penance and to fulfill other duties.

Slater noted the "very abundant" literature of devotional theology, but added that "moral theology proposes to itself the much humbler but still necessary task of defining what is right and what wrong in all the practical relations of the Christian life. . . . The first step on the right road of conduct is to avoid evil."[6]

From the fifth century to the Second Vatican Council, almost all moral instruction by moral theologians was to help priests judge about appropriate penances. Thus, when Mahoney claims that the sources of moral theology are in the penitential practices, there is a great deal of evidence and reason for him to make this assertion. However, as we may know almost intuitively, the tradition of moral theology is much richer than mere manuals and strict guidelines.

ARE THE PENITENTIALS, CONFESSIONAL MANUALS, AND MORAL MANUALS ENOUGH?

Many questions arise: Should we look at the history of the moral tradition in such a restrained way? Can we not look at history as more developed, broader, with actually a variety of other resources? Were not Christians formed morally in a variety of different ways, not only by moral theologians and their penitential, confessional, or moral manuals? Were not the moral lives of Christians like Mary Magdalene, Martin of Tours, Gregory the First, Francis and Clare, Dominic, Thomas Aquinas, Catherine of Siena, Ignatius of Loyola, Francis Xavier, Teresa of Avila, Elizabeth of Hungary, Dorothy Day, and others formed by something other than these manuals and their authors? Did their moral wisdom come from these books of moral pathology?

If we want to learn the moral wisdom of our tradition, then we cannot look to a history that restrains us. We need to see history as resourceful, and we need to look elsewhere than the textbooks that moralists wrote (though we should not avoid looking at them completely). Indeed, the Second Vatican Council called us to rethink moral theology in its declaration on priestly formation, Optatam Totius, when it admonished moral theology that it "should draw more fully on the teaching of holy scripture and should throw light upon the exalted vocation of the faithful in Christ."[7]

To appreciate our tradition, I look on history not as a restraint but as a resource, and therefore turn to the other four key "texts" of traditional moral formation: the person of Jesus in the New Testament, the Ten Commandments in the catechism, the practice of the corporal works of mercy, and the development of the four cardinal virtues. In the history of the moral formation of Christians, these were the texts to which bishops, preachers, teachers, religious orders, lay associations, confraternities, and others regularly appealed in order to become fully moral persons. These texts were the sources for developing our moral wisdom.

Within these texts certain specific lessons have frequently arisen over the centuries that define more specifically the contents of our wisdom. Therefore, before examining the texts our teachers used, I examine the lessons we have learned on love, conscience, sin, and suffering. My colleague and the Gilbert Stark Professor at Yale University, Margaret Farley, argues that despite all the doubts we encounter in the postmodern world, love and suffering are two truly human experiences universally shared by people throughout the ages.[8] For Christians, I would add that the experiences of conscience and sin are two other certain realities of our lives. Together these four experiences and the lessons they teach are the most important in the history of Christian moral wisdom. This book is an invitation to explore these experiences and lessons more fully and to apply them to our daily lives.

I believe, then, that by reflecting on each of these texts and lessons, you and I can get into contact once again with the formative influences of the heritage we share. We can come once again to appreciate and understand what gives meaning to our lives and what enhances our relationships with friends and family. As we finish these nine chapters, realizing that by looking back we can better understand where we are, I turn to the concluding chapter to look ahead. There I conclude the book looking to the future and at leadership through the lens of hope.

PART I

THE LESSONS

Chapter One

LOVE

ORDINARY STORIES

Having just celebrated my fiftieth birthday, I think of a lot of the people whom I love. I think especially of my younger brother Bobby. He was born 360 days after I was. My parents always told me that he was my first birthday present. In our childhood, we got along rather well. As a child, I loved Bobby. But I was an odd child. Until I was four years old, I never talked in anything but gibberish. The pediatrician kept insisting that in due time I'd figure out a right way of talking. In the meantime, Bobby was my translator.

"Do you two want to go out?" my mom would ask. I would answer in my own way, but my mom and dad had no idea what I was saying. After I finished saying everything that I thought was important, my mom would turn to Bobby, who would tell her what he wanted and what I meant to say.

We grew up in Brooklyn. My dad was a cop, with two other side jobs: delivering newspapers and baked goods. My mom was busy raising five children, and having been trained as a secretary, she did a lot of contracted typing at home.

We were an ambitious working-class family with a tight regimen. My parents examined us every night on our homework, were active in several parish organizations, and still had time for TV and family events.

I remember my brother Bobby especially because every year come February, we had three birthdays in a row: my dad's on February 3, Bobby's on February 10, mine on February 15. During the second week of February, my parents would invite about a dozen of our friends to a rather creative birthday party. My folks always had a different party theme: circus clowns, pirates, farmers, and so on. These were imaginative events, complete with costuming, a great deal of care, and a lot of aluminum foil (amazing what the working class can do with aluminum foil to jazz up an event).

The party would be between the tenth and the fifteenth of February, when Bobby and I were literally the same age. These birthday parties continued into our early adolescence. They were more exciting than Christmas. It was not my birthday—I never celebrated a birthday alone—it was Bobby's and mine. And it was not on his birthday or mine, but in between, because it was ours. And Bobby and I were happy with that because we were best friends.

Bobby died at twenty-six. Since then, nothing makes me more conflicted than *my* birthday. For the first twelve years of my life, the happiest day was when we celebrated together. I can remember them easily. I miss him. I feel very incomplete in losing him. We were very much a pair.

My brother's death shattered us all. I won't dwell on that, but rather on the many lessons we subsequently learned from his death. One was the importance of declaring our love for one another. My dad and mom wondered whether we told one another clearly enough that we love one another. So they began the practice of concluding their phone call conversations with us by saying the words "I love you."

We have been doing that for years. Every phone call concludes with those words, not only those calls with my mom, but with my cousin Michael, my sisters, and my brother, and now my nephews and nieces. We do not say "good-bye." We say "I love you."

These are, of course, the same words that we heard of on September 11, 2001. On September 11 we were exposed to the first extraordinary accounts of the major concerns that people want to express when they suddenly, without any preparation, face immediate, unexpected death.

Aristotle taught us that the unexpected reveals the true person. Without the opportunity to think ahead, a surprise catches us off guard and our true instincts emerge. On September 11, we learned what is really important. In all those truly awe-full cell-phone conversations from passengers on the planes that became weapons and from inside the buildings that became morgues, we heard repeatedly the words "I love you." "Tell the children of my love." One extraordinary account after another told the same words. There was not any other comparable expression or interest conveyed. There are no records of people calling to express anger, hate, or resentment. As many incredibly healthy and successful people faced unexpected, imminent death, they almost all tried to do the same thing: they wanted to contact another, another so important, and express in their dying words "I love you."

They did not ask "Do you love me?" As they faced death and separation, as they were filled with panic imagining how they could ever escape from each of the 110 stories of the buildings, their frightened spirits paused for a moment and rolled out of themselves to another to say "I love you." The human spirit is extraordinary in moving beyond itself. The human spirit so clearly feels how incomplete it is that it moves relentlessly toward union with others.

Union

I love the word *union*. That is what I felt with Bobby. It is also what those people on September 11 were reaching out for as they faced death.

Thomas Aquinas used *union* to talk about charity. By charity, he said, we are in union with God, neighbor, and self (II.II.23). Union is what we feel when we love. It is what a couple feels, a sibling, a child, a parent, a friend feels; that union is the desire to deepen union with another. As the twin towers were about to fall, love—the search for union—was a more apparent concern than hatred for those who did this, than fear of what was about to happen. In the last minutes of their lives, love, union is what they wanted to experience.

My friend Doris Donnelly, the director of the Cardinal Suenens Center at John Carroll University, tells the story of a young woman on the flight that crashed into the Pentagon. When the passengers realized there was a problem onboard, many began using their cell phones and learned that the towers had been attacked by other planes. These terrified passengers understood that a similar fate awaited them. After making a call with her cell phone, an older woman offered it to the younger woman seated next to her. The younger woman called her mother. The mother stayed on the phone, telling her daughter that she would stay with her all the way, that she wanted her to see that she was holding her as she held her when she was a baby. She wanted her daughter not to be alone. She wanted her to know of the consolation of union. The mother, too, had the presence of mind to recognize the generosity and concern of the elderly woman; she wanted her daughter to know that the woman next to her cared for her and that she should care for the woman. In an extraordinary moment, not unlike that of Jesus's crucifixion, this woman was telling her daughter that she should see the nice woman as her mother and that the nice woman should see the young woman as her daughter. She stayed in union with the two of them until their deaths.

I tell these stories because when theologians start talking about love, it often loses its visceral sense. If we take the visceral meaning out of love, we sap it of its energy. We need to feel that sense of union. Union has a very deeply felt, passionate, emotionally invested, human meaning. Union is what we all seek.

About twelve years ago, my dad had a coronary crisis and needed emergency bypass surgery. The operation was somewhat successful, but only two months later their beautiful home on Long Island's north shore was destroyed in a fire. For the subsequent seven months, my parents lived in a motel as they had contractors rebuild their home, aiming to sell it and retire to Florida.

From Fordham University in the Bronx where I was teaching, I would drive out to Long Island several times a week to have dinner with them. It was always good. I wanted to be with them. Sometimes, though, my dad would be pushing it a little too hard. "Dad, slow down," I would say. "I just want to get out of this motel and down to Florida and sit on the beach holding your mother's hand." (Sadly, it never happened; Dad died of a heart attack shortly after they moved to Florida.)

The call to union, the experience that we have of wanting to be together is really extraordinary. It is deeply instinctive and existential. So let me conclude this section, on a lighter note, with another story about holding hands.

In 1982 I moved to Rome to do doctoral study for five years. I flew on a very cheap flight. I was sitting next to the window, and the people next to me were a married couple. He had been wounded in Sicily during World War II and left to die in a barn. Days later some people found him unconscious, near death. Now forty years later, he was flying with his wife to find the barn. He wanted to revisit this place. Her name was Marcella Clarke and she asked about me, and I remarked that I was a Jesuit. She responded that her cousin was a Jesuit from my province and his name was Tom Clarke. I told her that I knew him well, that I had just had dinner with him, and that he had an uncle who owned P.J. Clarke's, a famous New York saloon and my parents' favorite bar there. "My father's place!" said Marcella.

After seeing how familiar our worlds were, we hit turbulence. Not your regular turbulence, mind you—we were riding a roller coaster. We were bouncing all over the place. We were deathly afraid and the turbulence lasted several hours. What did we do? Marcella, seated between her husband and me, grabbed our hands. She was not doing it to comfort me and him, nor to be consoled by us. She simply realized that we needed to be holding on to one another. Soon I realized everyone around us was holding hands. Why? If the plane broke in two, would it keep us from being any less shattered? Would holding hands break the impact of our falling to our deaths? Rather than holding onto dear life by holding onto our seats, we wanted to hold on to one another.

Starting with Love

I teach an introductory course on moral theology, and during my fifteen years teaching it, I only recently learned to begin my course on the topic of love. Not only did I not begin with love, I never even taught a class on it.

For me, love was what the philosophers call "formal." God loves us; we love God; we are called to morality as a response to that love, so let's discuss morality. There was nothing on the experience of love or union—nothing felt, nothing spiritual. It was a principle. Love God. How do I love God? Follow God's law. Admittedly, like all Christians I acknowledged that love has always been the foundation of my life and, in particular, my ethical vision. I also recognized that love was charity and nothing more or less. But I took it all for granted.

I began my course on freedom, a freedom for God, church, and neighbor. I was basically following my mentor, Josef Fuchs, who said that the beginning of all morality depends on personal freedom or basic freedom, a freedom in grace to realize the call of Christ.[1] Many other moral theologians from Europe started the same way. They did this because of their own experience in World War II. With such oppressive movements like the Nazis in Germany and the Fascists in Italy and Spain, moral theologians realized that freedom was the foundation for being moral. No freedom, no ability to pursue the good. They did not understand freedom as a freedom to do whatever one wanted to do. Rather, freedom was what we needed to follow

Christ. Without the grace of freedom, we could not pick up our cross and follow Christ.

Pope John Paul II and Cardinal Joseph Ratzinger usually began their writings on morality with truth.[2] They talked about the need to base all ethics on truth. In many ways the tension between moral theologians and teachers of the moral magisterium has been the preference each side has for either freedom or truth. One is looking more at the person, the other more at moral objectivity.

When Cardinal Ratzinger became Pope Benedict XVI, however, he made it clear that he wanted his teachings to start on love. He promulgated his encyclical, Deus Caritas Est (*God Is Love*), on December 25, 2005, the first Christmas of his pontificate. In the opening paragraph, he summarizes his interest in making an encyclical on love his first one.

> In a world where the name of God is sometimes associated with vengeance or even a duty of hatred and violence, this message is both timely and significant. For this reason, I wish in my first Encyclical to speak of the love which God lavishes upon us and which we in turn must share with others.

Like the pope, I believe we need to start with the primacy of love and specifically the love of God. Why love?

If we start with love instead of freedom or truth, what happens? Why start discussions of morality and ethics with love? Let me give you three reasons—from the scriptures, theology, and the tradition rooted in human experience—for starting with the love of God.

First, the scriptures command it. Jesus teaches us that the two great commandments are to love God and the neighbor as oneself. Of course, Jesus is summing up the entire teaching of the law and the prophets. So, for instance, the Ten Commandments recognize the love and honor for God as the first commandment of all. On it depend all the other commandments. Knowing that the commandments were not imposed on us for God's pleasure, but rather for our benefit and our flourishment, by insisting on God's sovereignty, the first commandment makes our dependency on God the very foundation of our happiness.[3]

Second, the love of God precedes whatever else we discuss in theology, whether we speak temporally or metaphysically. For instance, love is how we understand God, for God is love. The German Jesuit theologian Karl Rahner tells us that because God is love, God is triune, for God needs to be in God's self more than one person in order to be love, for the lover needs the beloved. Love also explains the creation. Again, Rahner tells us that because God is love, God "needs" to love more than God's self.[4] For that reason God creates us so as to enter into love with us, to bring us into his kingdom. Love also is the ground of our redemption, for "God so loved the world that God gave God's one and only Son, that whoever believes in him shall not perish but have eternal life" (John 3:16). Love, too, is the way of our sanctification, for Jesus commanded us to love God, to love our neighbor, and to love ourselves. Finally, love is our goal, for in the kingdom we believe that we will be united forever with God and those who have gone before us. Thus, love is our understanding of God, creation, redemption, sanctification, and eschatological promise: Inasmuch as theology is the study of God, then love is the beginning and end of theology, for God is love.

Listen to how the First Letter of John comprehensively presents it:

> Dear friends, let us love one another, for love comes from God. Everyone who loves has been born of God and knows God. Whoever does not love does not know God, because God is love. This is how God showed God's love among us: God sent God's one and only Son into the world that we might live through him. This is love: not that we loved God, but that God loved us and sent his Son as an atoning sacrifice for our sins. Dear friends, since God so loved us, we also ought to love one another. . . .

God is love. Whoever lives in love lives in God, and God in them. In this way, love is made complete among us so that we will have confidence on the day of judgment, because in this world we are like God. . . .

We love because God first loved us. If anyone says, "I love God," yet hates one's brother or sister, that one is a liar. For anyone who does not love one's brother or sister, whom we have seen, cannot love God, whom we have not seen. And God has given us this command: Whoever loves God must also love their brother and sister (1 John 4: 7–11, 16–17, 19–21).

It's hard to argue with this. Loving God is the foundation of the moral life.

A third reason for beginning with the love of God is that human experience confirms that, unlike freedom or truth, love drives, animates, moves. It is what prompted the cell-phone calls on September 11, 2001, the handing over of the human spirit looking for union. Not only does love look for union, but it also moves us toward freedom and truth. Love, then, makes possible our search for a freedom for greater love and a truth to love rightly.

One of the most important works in moral theology in the twentieth century specifically turned to the tradition to confirm this truth from human experience. In *The Primacy of Charity in Moral Theology*,[5] Gérard Gilleman insisted that we need an experience-based moral theology that starts at the depths of our being. He turned to charity, the love of God dwelling in us, and there he tapped into the notion of spiritual or devotional theology nourishing the depths of our spirit. When we think of charity, Gilleman quoted Thomas Aquinas as saying, we must realize that the love of God is no less than the presence of the Holy Spirit in us. Herein we find the love of God, charity animating us. Gilleman also invokes Thomas in calling charity the mother of the virtues, again because it precedes all other virtues by animating them and giving them life.

Tradition constantly confirms this human experience of the love of God preceding all else. For instance, our tradition testifies, time and again, to the love of God as the foundation of the call to become a Christian. Of course, the paradigmatic conversion marked by love is Augustine's (354–430) own. Augustine, who converted to Christianity in his early thirties, insisted on the primacy of love—"Love and do as you will." He describes in the tenth book of the *Confessions* the deeply felt, passionate, visceral pursuit of the love of God:

> Late it was that I loved you, beauty so ancient and so new, late I loved you! And, look, you were within me and I was outside, and there I sought for you and in my ugliness I plunged into the beauties that you have made. You were with me and I was not with you. Those outer beauties kept me far from you, yet if they had not been in you, they would not have existed at all. You called, you cried out, you shattered my deafness: you flashed, you shone, you scattered my blindness: you breathed perfume, and I drew in my breath and I pant for you: I tasted, and I am hungry and thirsty: you touched me, and I burned for your peace.[6]

Augustine's conversion was a response to the love of God already within him. Similarly, the conversion of St. Paul, who also testified to the primacy of love, was a call of love. Of course, unlike Augustine, we do not have from Paul the description of his conversion in quite the poetry that Augustine provided, but for the great evangelizer who wanted nothing but Christ, certainly he understood Christ's call as nothing but love.

I first came to this insight not from the Letters of Paul—though it was always there—but in a painting by Caravaggio (1573–1610). To appreciate Caravaggio's painting, I want to compare it with an earlier one by Michelangelo (1475–1564).

In Michelangelo's *The Conversion of St. Paul* (1542–1545), God, accompanied by angels and saints, erupts from heaven and parts the sky, allowing heaven's light to fall tornado-like on the person of Paul. God intervenes directly onto a plain, sending Paul's horse and at least fifteen soldiers away in flight. In the lower left-hand corner of the canvas, an elderly, white-bearded, stunned Paul shields his face as he turns toward the light with his companion helping him to his feet. The painting is clearly about the power of God entering dramatically and definitively into human history.

In Caravaggio's *Conversion of Paul* (1600), there are only three figures—Paul, his horse, and Paul's companion tending to the horse. On a fairly dark background we see a youthful Paul, in vibrant passionate colors of orange, red, blue, and yellow, wearing armor, very handsome on his back, legs opened, eyes closed. The conversion is an ecstatic moment in which Paul is purely recipient of God's love. It has a deeply erotic tone. The horse and his companion do not flee but remain standing there, neither aware of what is happening to Paul. Only Paul in his deep interiority is receiving the Lord. He is in union with the Lord. This deep, internalized conversion clearly conveys that God is doing something to Paul.

In this painting, unlike Michelangelo's, God is not visible. God is present, nonetheless, but in Paul, because someone is doing something to Paul. Caravaggio captures Paul's experience, making sure that the agent we see active is not Paul but God. Thus, even though you see God in Michelangelo's, still your eyes move to Paul. In Caravaggio's, you see Paul, but you look for God.

This move by Caravaggio is insightful. The event is not Paul being turned around. The event is Paul becoming deeply attuned to the presence of the love of God in his life. Of course, only one who has known that experience could insist that love is the only thing that lasts.

The greatness of our tradition is that the love of God is not simply the beginning of the Christian's life, but the whole continuum of it. Thus, in the Church of Maria del Popolo, Caravaggio's *Conversion of Paul* hangs in front of his *Crucifixion of Peter*. Like Paul, Peter is on his back, but his back is on a cross, and while the stimulated Paul is completely clothed, the aging flesh of Peter is fairly exposed, but hardly erotic. Peter is looking at his hands, fastened to the cross. He inevitably recalls the questioning on the beach—"Do you love me?"—and the prediction that Peter, when he is old, shall stretch forth his hands and be led where he will not want to go (John 21:15–19). Now Peter is old and about to die for Jesus Christ.

In two paintings, Caravaggio captures the beginning and the end of the Christian life as a life living out of the love of God.

THE THREEFOLD LOVE

No presentation on love can conclude without saying something about the threefold love of God, self, and neighbor. So let us consider this triad.

No contemporary moral theologian has written more on love than my own colleague at Weston Jesuit School of Theology, Edward Vacek.[7] Vacek captures the fullness of the love of God by talking about love as *agape* (that is, the love for the beloved), love as *philia* (the love for the love or the union itself), and love as *eros* (the love that the lover experiences as lover). By bringing these together, Vacek captures the all-encompassing comprehensiveness of love.

Not surprisingly, whenever we talk about our response to God's love, we similarly use all-encompassing language. Jesus tells us that we are to love the Lord our God with our whole heart, our whole mind, our whole soul (Matt. 22:37–39). God expects nothing less and the tradition echoes that complete offering, whether in the prayer of St. Francis or St. Ignatius of Loyola's *Suscipe* (offering of oneself) prayer. Any response to the all-embracing love of God must be as exhaustively comprehensive as the offer itself. Thus the breathless love of God that Paul encounters is paralleled by the complete *Suscipe* of Peter.

Because of that comprehensiveness, Vacek argues that all persons have their flourishment in God and that if one were not to believe in God, and therefore not know the love of God, that person would be incomplete. Humans, Vacek insists, need the love of God to know the goodness of life. Without it, we are simply less.

Vacek wants to make clear, though, that the love we are to have for God is specifically for God, God's self. Vacek wants to counter those who see in neighbor love the only specific act of the love of God. In a way, Vacek hearkens us back to the preacher who sees the placard that announces "God is other people." The preacher remarks, "There is a comma missing in your sign: 'God is other, people'!"

Thus in prayer we encounter this specific exchange of divine and human love between God and the person. Prayer is about entering into union with God specifically—about experiencing that union, about encountering the love of God. Margaret Farley talks about this expression of love as an active receptivity.[8] That active receptivity is what we saw in the Caravaggio painting of Paul: Paul is actively receiving the love of God.

The great Baroque artist Giovanni Bernini (1598–1680) caught this active receptivity when he sculpted the extraordinary ecstasy of Teresa of Avila (1515–1582). Not unlike Paul's body, Teresa's body completely succumbs to the penetrating love of God that permeates and enlivens her entire body.

Frederick Crowe described this active receptivity in another word: "complacency."[9] There he describes the first act of the beloved as resting in the love received from the lover. Complacency and active receptivity is what we see in Caravaggio's Paul and Bernini's Teresa.

St. Ignatius of Loyola (1491–1556) is always leading us in prayer to appreciate complacency, this active receptivity. Ignatius always saw prayer as a way of receiving God, as being inflamed by God. As Ignatius directs us in prayer, he never lets us leave one scriptural passage for another, if there is still more fruit to savor.

I remember, for instance, an eight-day retreat that I began on Romans 8. I was so moved by that extraordinary chapter on hope and the Holy Spirit that when I saw my spiritual director the second day, he told me to repeat my five prayer periods on Romans 8. I enjoyed those periods and returned for each of the eight days to the same passage. Complacency is that active reception, that encounter with the indwelling of the Holy Spirit.

The genius of Ignatius is that he couples that experience of complacency with the comprehensiveness of love: he wants us to get at complacency from every imaginable angle. From meditations, colloquies, contemplations, and the applications of the senses, Ignatius wants us to see, feel, touch, hear, and taste the love of God.[10]

Like the love of God itself, prayer is an encounter with being beloved. Thus Thomas Aquinas had the great insight to write that the order of charity begins with God and moves to the self (II.II.26). After our encounter with the love of God, we love ourselves. God teaches us to do it, and even before we love another, we believe that by charity we love ourselves and well we should.[11]

Of course, the Gospels make this quite clear: the model for neighbor love is love of self; we are to love the neighbor as ourselves. Here is the richness of the Christian tradition on love: the love of God makes possible the love of self. And these together make possible the love of neighbor.

I think it is important to understand here a common mistake many make. Many seem to think that love of self is conditioned by whether we think of ourselves as good first. I do not want to dwell here on how good or bad we are—wait until my chapter on sin to see how "bad" I think we are—but we acknowledge in faith that while we were still sinners, God loved us (Rom. 5:8). God does not love us in our goodness; God loves us in our entirety.

I have told this story before in two other books of mine, but it is worth telling again, because in it, I discovered at once what a sinner I am and how loved I am, and I felt in that same moment how much I could love myself.

From 1982 to 1987 I studied at the Gregorian University in Rome. During the summer, I would travel to either Germany or Austria for part-time study of the German language and part-time parish work. One summer, while living in Munich, I decided to go to Dachau. I wanted to go on one particular Monday, knowing that, like most European museums, the one at the camp would be closed. I wanted to go to Dachau only to pray, and I had heard that I could pray at a convent chapel that a group of religious women maintained next to the camp. In my Jesuit community in Munich, one of the members was the sisters' chaplain and he informed me that I could pray there, even on Mondays, when the camp was closed. Thus, I set out one cloudy day on my journey to pray at Dachau.

Foregoing a bus that could have taken me directly there from the train station, I walked to the camp for about three or four miles. As I walked, I became more and more angry. All I saw were nice, suburban houses with manicured lawns. I saw no trace of the tragedy of Dachau. I started asking myself, *How could anyone after 1945 live in a city called Dachau? What type of people could have a mailing address identical to the place of such persecution?* I thought that if ghosts existed, they would surely haunt this town. As I soon saw the cinderblock camp ahead of me, I wondered how anyone could claim seriously not to have known about the killings. I got closer, the skies were dark, and off to the side of the main street that led to the camp, I saw a new, white, Alpine-looking church. I thought, who are these people of Dachau who could claim that God was here in this place where they conspired to kill so many Jews, gypsies, homosexuals, and others?

I got to the camp. I was surprised by its length as I walked alongside it, and when I finally reached the end, I found the bell of the convent and rang it. I soon heard a voice telling me in German that the convent was closed. I responded that I was not a tourist, that I came only to pray. "We're closed," the German sister repeated. "I'm a Jesuit and your chaplain told me that I could pray here." "We're closed." "Can't I pray?" "We're closed; it's Monday."

I had come to Dachau to pray and was not allowed to. I began my trek back, even angrier than before. The skies were darker and my spirits were enraged. As I walked back, I saw the white church again. I thought, I did not come to pray in the church where conspirers pray;

I came to pray where the persecuted died. I would not pray there in that white church.

I thought, nonetheless, that I had come to Dachau to pray. Here I had an opportunity to pray. Should I avoid the very point of my journey? I crossed the road and entered the white church. I looked up at the altar, and there I saw it. Suspended over the altar was an enormous corpus of the suffering Christ, crucified not to wood, but to the very barbed wire that the people of this town had once made for the camps. There was the suffering Christ, the Jew, and His cross had been fashioned by the Catholics of this town. They knew their guilt. And with as much speed as it took for me to see the barbed wire, I knew my guilt as well.

I had come as an innocent to pray for the dead; there in the church I saw that I was guilty.

I sat down, stunned. For one hour I sat overthrown by my own guilt, wickedness, and sinfulness. I was awash in it. And yet, I did not feel any depression. I felt, instead, light. I felt that somehow Christ wanted me to know myself, my pettiness, my selfishness, my seething judgment, and would not let me be shattered by the knowledge. I was overcome by my badness and yet Christ's strength, light, and, yes, love would not let me be lost. I felt extraordinarily vulnerable, yet oddly confident, not in me, but in Christ.

After an hour or so, I prayed for all the people that my selfishness had harmed. I begged their forgiveness and I thanked God for this revelation of myself and of God's tender love. I left the church. Outside, I looked up, the skies were beautifully blue, with wisps of clouds across the horizon. Then a little boy passed by on his tricycle, saw me, and uttered the wonderful Bavarian greeting: "Grüss Gott!" He had just said to me, "God's greetings!" I sat down on the curb and cried. And in my tears, I realized how worthwhile it was to love God, myself, and my neighbor.

I conclude now on neighbor love. Like my experience at Dachau, we cannot love our neighbors except for as they are. I learned, in my sinfulness, by God's love, what self-love was. The comprehensiveness of love is no less applicable for neighbor love. We are called to love our neighbors, not in their goodness alone but in their entirety and in their specificity.

There are some today who try to love their neighbor by thinking of their neighbor as another Christ. But I think that is not full neighbor love: we need to love not Christ in the neighbor only, but we need also to love the neighbor. Just as we need to love specifically God and specifically ourselves, similarly we need to love specifically our neighbors as they really are. Moreover, just as we love ourselves as we really are, so too we are to love our neighbors as ourselves.

I do not want to deny that Christ may reveal to us that *after* loving our neighbor we may discover Christ, but I think that the tradition has always told the story of finding Christ in my neighbor as a lesson learned *after* the concrete act of loving the neighbor. In the Last Judgment parable in Matthew 25, we hear the sheep being told that because they fed the King, they will enter the Kingdom of God. Then they ask, "When did we feed *you?*" and the King answers, "Whenever you fed the hungry, you fed me." In the Christian tradition, St. Martin of Tours gives his cloak to a beggar in need. Later, he realizes that the beggar was Christ. But in both Matthew's Gospel and in the story of Martin, each one acts not because they see Christ, but because they see a neighbor in need. It is one thing to love Christ in Jack; it is another matter to love Jack.

I close by reflecting on prayer. For just as in prayer we encounter the love of God and the experience of active receptivity wherein we know we are loved and called to love ourselves, similarly in prayer we practice neighbor love, especially when we pray for one another. Again, in this practice we learn to love again as we enter into union with one another by lifting each other up in prayer.

We learn in prayer and from the Gospels how much God wants us to love one another, and God becomes in prayer and in life the guarantor of that love. God makes that love possible and therefore never attempts to replace that love we have for another with our love for God. When we learn lessons in love, we learn not to reduce love, but that love's nature is to extend itself, to reach beyond the self, to grasp the other, again and again, and another and another. Love is, after all, union—a deeply felt, visceral union that we keep pursuing and keep preserving in a multitude of ways, for it is so comprehensive and yet brings such complacency.

Study Questions

If you were teaching a course on moral theology, where would you start? Love? Freedom? God? Human experience? The church? Jesus Christ? Why would you start where you propose?

Do you think we can love God without loving our neighbor? Do you think we can love our neighbor without loving God?

Do you think everyone needs to love God?

How would you describe love?

Chapter Two

CONSCIENCE

Hᴏᴡ ᴍᴀɴʏ ᴛɪᴍᴇꜱ ʜᴀꜱ ᴀ ꜱᴘᴏᴜꜱᴇ ꜰᴏᴜɴᴅ ᴛʜᴀᴛ ᴛʜᴇ ɢʀᴇᴀᴛᴇꜱᴛ trouble in a marriage is due to the other spouse's immaturity? How many pastors know that the most time-consuming difficulties they face are with a childish staff member? How many religious communities are held hostage by the expectations of one spoiled member? How many friendships are strained by the indulgent urges of someone who has never outgrown adolescence? Or better yet, let us consider ourselves. How many of us know that our worst moments result when our juvenile propensities continue to influence us?

THE CALL TO GROW

The call to be a Christian is at once a call to grow. This seemingly obvious yet healthy maxim is not, however, readily found in the long history of the moral manuals that constantly warn us against sin without urging us to grow. The call to grow is evident elsewhere: in the scriptures, in the early Fathers, in the twelfth- to fourteenth-century Scholasticism and the concurrent charismatic and religious movements, and finally again in our contemporary era.

In the New Testament, the call to follow the Lord is always understood as a call to advance. Saint Paul writes, "forgetting what lies behind and straining forward to what lies ahead, I press on toward the goal for the prize of the upward call of God in Christ Jesus" (Philem. 3:13–14). The ever-moving Paul finds appropriate the imagery of straining forward on the way of the Lord. To the Galatians he laments their stumbling and comments "you were running well" (Gal. 5:7).

Paul's reliance on journey imagery stems from his own confirming experience of Christ, who literally manifests his love to Paul as Paul journeys toward Damascus to persecute Christ's followers. Paul is a traveler, both before and after his conversion. After meeting the risen Lord, Paul is sent on the true way. Paul's actual journeys, narrated in Luke's Acts of the Apostles, mirror the Gospel journeys of Christ, who heads for Jerusalem. They are both being called to their ultimate surrender.

Following in Jesus's footsteps is the response to the call of discipleship: the first traveler, the Lord himself, beckons each pilgrim to advance by following him. The provocative Italian film director Pier Paolo Pasolini (1922–1975) brought the journeying of Jesus to the fore in his *The Gospel According to Saint Matthew*. In that work he silhouettes Jesus as Jesus moves relentlessly across the screen toward Jerusalem, with his apostles trying desperately but rather poorly to keep up with him. Jesus is on a mission, aiming without pause to attain his destiny; everything that he does, he does as he makes haste to the Holy City. Even his Sermon on the Mount becomes a sermon on the run.

Of course, the notion of movement originates with the Gospels and not with Pasolini. The Gospels are replete with "moving" characters, seeking the Lord: the shepherds hurry to the stable as the Magi follow the star, Zacchaeus climbs a tree and Levi leaves his table, the woman with the hemorrhage pushes through the crowd and the paralytic finds the Lord by entering through a roof, the prodigal son and his father rush toward one another, Jairus and Nicodemus break ranks to see Jesus, and Cornelius visits Peter. The Gospels are filled with stories of people literally striding in their passage to the Lord.

The scripture stories were not lost on the church. The stories became the source of a new moral imperative: to advance. Gregory the Great (540–604; papacy, 590–604) wrote, "Certainly, in this world, the human spirit is like a boat foolishly fighting against the river's rush: one is never allowed to stay still, because unless one forges ahead, one will slide back downstream."[1] Later, in the twelfth century, Bernard of Clairvaux (1090–1153) argued, "To not progress on the way of Life is to regress."[2] Thomas Aquinas (1225–1274) summed up their insights: "To stand on the way of the Lord is to move backwards."[3] For them, the Lord who leads us on the way expects us to move, to follow. To not follow is to retreat.

This moral call to grow is not a call to make ourselves into other gods. Certainly some have erroneously believed that by their own efforts they could become perfect, like those who ate from Eden's tree, who built the Tower of Babel, or who followed the Bishop Pelagius. But Paul helps us again: "Not that I have obtained this or am already perfect; but I press on to make it my own, because Christ Jesus has made me his own" (Philem. 3:12). The call to strive, to grow, is not a matter of choice. Rather, Christ has called us and given us the grace that commands us to respond. On God's account, we must move forward.

All this movement would be lost on us if we did not understand it as being out of love. Out of love Jesus moves to the Father in Jerusalem; out of love Paul races to the finish line; out of love Mary hastens to her cousin Elizabeth; out of love Peter and John rush to the empty tomb; out of love Mary Magdalene runs ahead to tell the disciples about the risen Lord. This call to movement, to advance, is the Christian call to grow, but to grow in love.

RIGHT GROWTH, RIGHT LOVING, AND THE PROMOTION OF THE CONSCIENCE

This call to grow in love is a summons to pursue the right way for growing. For this reason the call to growth often becomes an injunction to cultivate the virtues. By concentrating on virtues or character building, we can attend to practices that better our pilgrimage. Though virtues assist us to harness weaknesses and overcome pitfalls, their overriding function is to develop strengths. The agenda of the virtues is to promote a profoundly interpersonal and positive response to the call to grow and stands in sharp contrast to the later modern moral manuals that were so obsessed with avoiding sinful actions.

This connection between the Gospels and the virtues appears in the history of the church, not only in the patristic period but also in the great charismatic movements of the twelfth and thirteenth centuries, especially in the challenging summons of Saints Dominic (1170–1221), Francis (1181–1226), and Clare (1194–1253) to walk on the way of the Lord. Unlike their predecessors, who lived in remote monasteries, these charismatic leaders frequently left their convents to enter the newly formed urban areas and universities of the thirteenth century so as to preach the Gospel, forming religious communities precisely for that task. Telling the story of God's movement to us, they call us to move today toward God on the way of virtue.

The call to grow, the call to move forward as disciples, the call to put on virtue is always a call heard in the Christian conscience. The centrality of the personal conscience as the place for hearing the call has had a long history in the church: whenever growth and virtue are especially promoted, the conscience is also defended and promoted. During these robust periods (notably the patristic period of the first five centuries and the charismatic, religious, and Scholastic movements of the twelfth to fourteenth centuries), the primacy of the conscience is consistently articulated. Not surprisingly, then, in light of the reforms of the Second Vatican Council, which called morals to be more rooted in scripture and discipleship, the conscience again makes a vigorous appearance in contemporary moral theology.

What does Vatican II say about conscience? The definitive presentation is paragraph 16 of Gaudium et Spes:

In the depths of our conscience, we detect a law which does not impose, but which holds us to obedience. Always summoning us to love good and avoid evil, the voice of conscience when necessary speaks to our heart: do this; shun that. For we have in our heart a law written by God; to obey it is the very dignity of being human; according to it we will be judged (2 Cor. 6:10). Conscience is the most secret core and sanctuary of a person. There we are alone with God, Whose voice echoes in our depths (John 1:3, 14). In a wonderful manner conscience reveals that law which is fulfilled by love of God and neighbor (Eph. 1:10). In fidelity to conscience, Christians are joined with the rest of humanity in the search for truth, and for the genuine solution to the numerous problems which arise in the life of individuals from social relationships. Hence the more right conscience holds sway, the more persons and groups turn aside from blind choice and strive to be guided by the objective norms of morality. Conscience frequently errs from invincible ignorance without losing its dignity. The same cannot be said for those who care but little for truth and goodness, or for a conscience which by degrees grows practically sightless as a result of habitual sin.

There are many elements that we could pursue here—the inner sanctuary of a person, the call to do good and avoid evil, the law being fulfilled in the love of God and neighbor—but so as to explain conscience better I want to examine only three specific issues: the "voice" of conscience, the formation of conscience, and the erring conscience.

The Voice of Conscience

In a seminal article thirty years ago, John Glaser distinguished two very different voices that we hear as adults: the voices of the superego and of the conscience. The term "superego" (meaning "that-which-is-over-the-I") is how psychologists name that voice living in us, which, though a leftover from early childhood years, continues to assert itself throughout our lives.

When we were young children, those who cared for us instructed us on matters of safety and hygiene. Our parents through persistent guidance kept us from running in front of cars, putting our fingers into electrical outlets, playing with knives, or turning on the oven. Similarly, they taught us to keep clean, wash our hands, eat with utensils, and use the toilet. These instructions were given through voices of authorities spoken with great concern and often, understandably, with tones of stress and frustration. Subsequently, these voices formed the voice of the superego.

Because they could not be omnipresent, parents and guardians needed to instill in us a voice that could supervise us even in their absence. Through constant warnings, we eventually felt their inhibiting presence restraining us from pushing a playmate in front of traffic or from exploring the many dangerous appliances in the kitchen. As children we learned that parents were always nearby. In fact, nothing could make parental control more palpably visible than when that horrendous sibling threat was uttered: "Wait 'til I tell Mom!"

Glaser calls this internalized supervising voice "a principle of pre-personal censorship and control."[4] It still lives in us today. Unfortunately, inasmuch as this voice came from people literally bigger and older than we children were, we still perceive this voice as more powerful and more authoritative than we are.

The superego was not, however, a moral guide. It was simply meant to restrain us, to keep us safe, healthy, and well. Despite whatever moral lessons parents may have given us during this time, the only thing we children really heard was that if we did not heed our parent's instructions, we would get punished. The threat—not nice moral explanations—is what we remember.

When we were wrong, we were punished, most often by being sent to our room. This is the paradigmatic form of reprimanding a child. At first we delighted in being sent away; our rebellious streak was awakened by the punishment. We thought as we stomped our way to our room, good riddance! As time passed, we would feel, however, the intended isolation and would seek permission to return to wherever the family was gathered. We would negotiate with our parents, promising never to be bad again, and claiming to be contrite all along the way. Of course, we were not that upset about the wrong we had done; it was the isolation we wanted to overcome. We wanted to be back with everyone and feel loved again.

Today that same fairly standardized cyclic movement has been hardwired into our adult lives. From the superego we sense reprimand, punishment, isolation, guilt, negotiation, repentance, and acceptance. Through the superego, the cycle repeats itself time and again. We violate an accepted standard of behavior, we feel "guilty" for what we did, we apologize simply to rid ourselves of the "bad" feeling, and we are welcomed back, and we find ourselves feeling better again. Such are the mechanics of the superego.

THE FORMATION OF THE CONSCIENCE

Unlike the superego, which warns us to stay where we are, the conscience calls us to grow. For some of us, this call could mean a call to greater assertiveness. Given the call to grow, we may hear another voice warning us, "You better not do it or else you will feel guilty." That guilt-inducing voice is usually the superego. Often the conscience's calls to grow are met with threats of the superego. Even if we do decide to develop in new areas, the superego still manages to make us feel guilty and, worse, terribly isolated. Some of us even go to our rooms, punishing ourselves exactly as our parents punished us years ago.

When I lived as a faculty-in-residence in Fordham University dorms, I saw hard-driving, bright students who, whenever they received anything less than an A, retreated to their rooms and went into a period of mourning, invariably calling their parents to be cheered up. When the superego drives us, it usually does so by threatening or punishing us, compelling us into prepubescent cyclic forms of living and acting.

Certainly this is not to say that whenever we "feel guilty," the superego and not the conscience is working. When we say things like "I feel so guilty," we should ask ourselves, "Did I do anything wrong?" If the answer is yes, then the conscience is probably judging us, but when the answer is no, the superego is probably intimidating us. Consider the case that someone has repeatedly treated us poorly. Our friends suggest, "You should speak up and tell that person to stop taking advantage of you." In conscience we recognize that this is what we should do, but the superego keeps saying, "You should be a nice person." Eventually we decide to speak up. Afterward, we may "feel guilty." This feeling is probably rooted in the superego: we went against its command to be nice and so it punished us.

Of course, the superego is not bad. After all, because of it we do not run in front of cars or play with electrical outlets, and we, thankfully, use the toilet and wash our hands. However, during our adult lives we have to live by a higher voice (the conscience) that discerns the standards of what is right and wrong. In short, we need to be vigilant about the superego so that it does not inhibit the conscience.

Moreover, by the superego we experience a certain form of social compliance. Because we are so interested in being loved, the superego threatens us with isolation and therefore harkens us always to conformity. Conscience, on the other hand, is suspicious of conformity, particularly when injustice is at stake. Because the conscience calls us to aim more at being the one who loves than being the beloved, it prompts us often to reach out to the one that the more conformist society rejects. Moral progress, therefore, always occurs when people heed their consciences, take steps of their own, and move forward, even at the risk of isolation and loss. Consider when Rosa Parks took her place on the bus in Montgomery, when Thomas More refused to take the Oath of Supremacy, when Martin Luther King Jr. wrote to white preachers on scraps of paper in a Birmingham jail, when Gdansk shipyard workers decided to strike for their rights, when the faceless Chinese student stepped forward to meet an oncoming tank in Tiananmen Square, or when Ninoy Aquino returned to his beloved Philippines. In each instance, a person moved history and humanity forward with a conscience that demanded stepping forward where others feared to go.

Here we should never forget that the language of conscience is the forceful language of being called, of being commanded. As Gaudium et Spes states, conscience "holds us in obedience"—it "summons" us. True, conscience is often used with the word "freedom," but this is not a freedom to do whatever we want. Rather, the call for freedom of conscience is so that we are not constrained from heeding our conscience. For this reason, Christians refer to the "dictates" or the "demands" of conscience: conscience "demands" that we love God, ourselves, and our neighbors. Conscience "dictates" that we pursue justice. In fact, Gaudium et Spes reminds us that by the conscience we will be "judged."

When we appreciate the call of conscience, the voice to hear the demands of God, of love, and of justice, then we similarly recognize the formation of the conscience as itself a command. We need to remember, however, that forming our conscience is a lifetime process. We form it based on the wisdom of parents, elders, and teachers, as well as friends and mentors; on the teachings and stories from the sacred scriptures, the church's tradition, and our local culture; and finally on the lessons learned in our own life experience.

Many people think that forming the conscience entails learning a few laws, like the Ten Commandments. These are certainly helpful and important but we need to learn life's lessons if we want to have a formed conscience, and those lessons cannot be taught by simple commands telling us what to do and what to avoid.

The formation of conscience is like parenting oneself. We can think of how our parents helped us to begin forming our consciences, since parents form their children's consciences all the time. They teach their children to play fairly with others, to enjoy one another's company, to tell the truth, to care for siblings and friends, to take care of themselves by not eating too much or too quickly, to respect other people's property, and to be brave.

As we get older and become adults, we take over the job of forming the conscience. We learn more about the complexities of truth-telling, of being faithful to friends, of acknowledging our faults, of working earnestly, of caring for the stranger, of being hospitable, and of becoming both grateful and compassionate.

I think the formation of the conscience is really a development of our relatedness in virtue: mentored practices of justice, temperance, fortitude, fidelity, and self-care through the ministration of conscience's own prudence allow us to learn more and more about how we are to respond to God, neighbor, and ourselves in love. Virtuous practices become the exercises for the formation of conscience.

The seriousness with which the church takes the conscience is seen by the way the church addresses the possible conflict between the dictates of conscience and the teaching church. What happens if my conscience tells me one thing and my church tells me something else?

This was the famous disagreement that the young Thomas Aquinas had with the famous Peter Lombard (1095–1160). Peter Lombard's *Sentences* was the most widely used textbook (after the scriptures) of the medieval university. Every budding professor lectured on them as their first university lecture appointment. In 1252, when Thomas Aquinas first arrived at Paris to teach, he did the same. Thomas dutifully referred to Lombard as the Master, but on three occasions in his *Commentary on the Sentences*, Thomas straightforwardly rejected Lombard: "here the Master is wrong" (*hic magister falsum dicit*). Lombard had argued that one is not obliged to follow one's conscience when at odds with church teaching. Thomas responded that we ought to die excommunicated rather than violate our conscience.[5]

We need to appreciate that the "debate" between Peter and Thomas was never settled. No pope or council ever judged that Peter or Thomas was right. Rather, in the church we live with the tension of this debate. In fact, generally speaking we believe that to form the conscience we should adhere to church teaching. We expect the conflict between conscience and church teaching to be rare. In fact, we could say that the only way we could in conscience disagree with church teaching is if our consciences took the matter so seriously that it commanded us to disagree with the church.

Still, I believe that Thomas understood the problem well: if we are not bound to what our conscience dictates as right, then we would be free to follow any fancy as morally right. But we are bound to the dictates of conscience. In fact, on Judgment Day we will have to give an account of how we lived and that account will be based on conscience. We will not be able to claim we were following others, for even the act of following is itself a conscientious action. There will be no excuses; inevitably we will render the account of how we lived and why. In being true to our lives, we will have no choice but to acknowledge how our consciences guided us throughout our adult lives. Thus, even if we believe we ought to adhere to church teaching, we do that through conscience. The conscience, then, is the seat of personal responsibility.

Following the conscience is not a private matter. On the contrary, as the seat of personal responsibility, it helps us to see that we are constitutively related to God, ourselves, and the neighbor. We are inescapably social, so much so that whatever our conscience guides us to do will be brought to light. Whatever we try to do in private will inevitably enter into the very nature of ourselves. Since we cannot escape our consciences, we cannot escape our own relational responsibilities.

Moreover, because conscience always binds, it binds even when it is erroneous; of course, no one in conscience would know that they were in error, for deliberately doing what we believe is wrong would not be acting in conscience.

Few moral teachings of the church must be followed under pain of excommunication. Nonetheless, if the church teaches one thing and we believe in conscience something else, we are obliged to know what exactly the church teaches and whether we still have grounds for disagreement. Then we ought to know exactly what the disagreement is and how serious it is, and articulate to ourselves precisely why we are convinced that our way of acting is the more obliging way of loving God and neighbor than what the church teaches. In all of this, we must maintain a profound respect for the church's teaching and we must avoid scandalizing others. But the only reason why in this conflict we are obliged not to obey the church is because we are absolutely not free to violate our conscience.

Still, just because we follow our conscience does not mean that we are right. As a matter of fact, when we think about it, it is pretty easy to get things wrong. The recognition of the obligation to follow our conscience, then, does not mean that we become infallible if we heed the conscience. On the contrary, as Gaudium et Spes acknowledges, "conscience frequently errs."

For that reason it is important to ask the question: Do we sin when we follow a conscience in error? This question has been asked since the twelfth century, and over time, we have developed different answers.

THE ERRONEOUS CONSCIENCE

I turn now to the debate on the erroneous conscience because, by studying it, we can appreciate more clearly the primacy of the conscience. Moreover, by studying these different theologians we get a sense of what we mean when we say that the tradition develops. Here on the question of the erroneous conscience we see the church's theology going forward.[6]

Before we study these theologians, we need to recognize a distinction in moral theology between goodness and rightness. Goodness pertains to the person's basic moral stance. It asks: Do we love or do we strive for the right action? Rightness refers to whether the action fulfills the standards of ethics. Good people strive to get their actions right but do not always succeed. People acting out of selfishness might well do the morally right action, but since they do not act out of love, we do not refer to them as good.[7]

With these distinctions we equate badness with sin. Sin is the opposite of goodness: we can call it the failure to bother to love, a definition to which we will return in the next chapter.

Bernard of Clairvaux (1090–1153), distrusting human judgment and believing that the root of sin was ignorance, exhorted his listeners to the virtue of humility and adherence to the law. Actions contrary to the law and its teaching, even though done out of ignorance, were, according to Bernard, in a word, bad. Thus, if we accept that telling a lie is always wrong, Bernard would say, if we told a lie, regardless of our motivation, we sinned.

Peter Abelard (1079–1142) thought differently. He taught that what mattered was whether we were willfully pursuing in conscience the truth. Thus, if we told a lie in conscience in order to protect ourselves, Abelard would call us and our action good. Thus, faced with our question, whether an action from a sincerely erroneous conscience is a sin, Bernard answers affirmatively, and Abelard negatively.

The debate between them occurred, I think, because the two great theologians were each using only one concept to describe two completely different concerns. Bernard failed to see that just because persons may do the wrong out of error does not necessarily mean that they are at fault and therefore sinful. Abelard wrote about moral motivation. Our motivations may be out of love and conscience, but conscience and love are no guarantee that actions will be morally right. If we willed something precisely because we thought it to be right, Abelard would call our action right.

Think if you were to arrive home tonight and someone met you at the door saying "Now I have something to tell you. Before you say anything, you should know, he did it out of love." Are those "comforting" words or "warning" words? Do you think something good is actually waiting for you inside? I don't think so. Acting out of love or out of conscience is not a guarantee of right acting. Thus, whenever we hear someone say "he did it out of love" or "she meant well," we know something terribly wrong has happened, but that the person did not mean for it to be wrong. On the contrary, they were trying to find the right. Thus, if our conduct stemmed from an erroneous conscience, we may have been seeking the right, but we did not find it.

Later in life, Thomas Aquinas entertained the question about whether a person is good when following an erroneous conscience. Thomas's question concerned sincerity and striving: Regarding the error, he asked, could one have known otherwise? For example, I believe I should enlist in the army and fight in a war. I later learn that the war was unjust. Am I responsible for my error? Thomas would ask me, could I have known the war was unjust before participating in it? If the answer was yes, then I was responsible for the erroneous conscience; if no, then I was not responsible. Thomas would call my action of enlistment wrong, but whether my action was a sin depends on whether I tried to know what I needed to know.

But what would Thomas say if I wrestled with the question of the war and then enlisted precisely because, after investigation, I believed firmly that this was a just and necessary war? Would Thomas say that though my action was wrong, I was good? Curiously, Thomas did not call the person good who, despite striving to know the right, followed an erroneous conscience; rather, Thomas argued that such a person is "excused" from blame.

Later, William of Ockham (1350) adopted Thomas's argument on the primacy of the conscience but added that one who exercises the conscience responsibly, even if it is erroneous, receives merit. Ockham, unlike Abelard, recognized that ignorance is sometimes blameworthy but, like Abelard, he recognized the goodness of an erroneous conscience acting in good faith.

Certainly by the sixteenth century most moral theologians agreed with Thomas—that a dictate of conscience must be followed and that an erroneous conscience in good faith is, at least, excused from blame. In fact, by the end of the seventeenth century in 1690, Pope Alexander VIII condemned all those who taught that an invincibly ignorant conscience did not, at least, excuse. (Implicitly, Bernard's attack on Abelard is rejected.)

In the eighteenth century, Alfonso Liguori (1787), later the patron saint of moral theologians, developed a new position on erroneous conscience: if a person acted out of love and/or charity when committing error, then not only is the person excused, but the person is good. Whereas Ockham described the person's striving as meritorious, now Liguori, in many ways the master of the moral manuals, asserts the person's goodness.

In the nineteenth and twentieth centuries, the moral manualists endorsed Liguori's teaching. For instance, in speaking of when a person acting from an erroneous conscience would be good, they gave the specific example of lying to protect someone. Thomas's hesitancy to describe any wrongdoer as good was overcome by Liguori and adopted by his successors. In 1953, Francis Connell, the dean of Catholic University in Washington, D.C., wrote that if a person acts out of an erroneous conscience, though the action is certainly not *per se* willed by God, "God will reward him for sincerely following his conscience."[8]

CONCLUSION

What can we conclude about this development of theological opinion on erroneous conscience? First, the description of the sincere but ignorant conscience as bad is justly condemned by Pope Alexander VIII.

Second, to describe erroneous actions as "good" is likewise rejected. Trying to find the right is no guarantee of eventual success.

Third, some may feel inclined to accept Thomas's description of the person as "excused." But today we use "excused" to describe a person who is victimized by some external cause that diminishes the ability to will and act. Thus, under the control of mental illness, drugs, threats, and so on, a person would be "excused" from blame today, if that control resulted through no fault on the person's part.

If a person has been first acting out of love or out of conscience, searching to find the right, then the person is good. Unlike being coerced or drugged, a person who errs in good faith is a person who has struggled to find the right, searched heart and mind, and in firm good faith and free will acted with conviction, albeit in error. This person is good, and what differentiates this person from another who strives in the same way but whose conduct is recognized as right is precisely the evaluation of the conduct as wrong. Calling the conduct wrong is the sufficient negative description for the activity of the erroneous conscience.

One evident instance where getting things right is an arduous and unlikely event is parenting. This vocation requires getting things right for oneself as well as for one's children, who themselves are unpredictable. Thus, in teaching children responsibility, parents often miss the mark. But why? Do parents err because they were, at that moment, less loving or less conscientious? Or do they err from a lack of experience, or foresight, or, let us say, perfect knowledge?

When a parent tries to get things right, he or she may fail. But does that failure result from the parent loving less? The parent was wrong, admittedly, but in the care and striving to do the right, to help and instruct the child, was the parent less loving? If there was no diminishment in the striving for the right, there was no diminishment in the moral goodness. Thus calling the conduct wrong does not mean that the parent was any less good or loving than another who strove equally as much and gave the right guidance.

Still you may not want to draw the same conclusions. Such hesitancy may result from two objections. The first, you may be thinking: "Are you saying that Hitler, because he may have acted out of conscience, was not bad?" But we have to ask, do we really believe that Hitler was striving as much as possible to find the right? Do we really believe that, in a world that has taught for centuries that injustice is wrong and has tried to elucidate the most minimal insights into justice, Hitler's activities were simply mistaken and sincere interpretations of justice? Can we really believe a scenario in which the

Holocaust is the thinking of a person who was striving to be right? Certainly the access we have to any of the discussions leading to his decisions hardly supports such a belief. In a word, the Hitler question only proves our insight: not only was Hitler's conduct wrong, but his motivations were bad or evil. In the case of Hitler, his evident failure to strive for justice was so appallingly clear that we rightfully call him bad. As Iris Murdoch writes, "we have not recovered from . . . the experience of Hitler."[9] But Hitler and other unjust dictators aside, the contemporary reflection on erroneous conscience helps us to see something often overlooked: the failure to act rightly does not result necessarily from a failure to act out of conscience.

Still, some may want to keep Thomas's evaluation for another reason. After all, our record (as individuals and as a people) for getting things wrong is strikingly high. With such a record we are wary of any device that could diminish our efforts. We sense that if we start calling these well-meaning wrongdoers good, we'll let them off the hook.

But is it not more often the case that the last people to let themselves "off the hook" are precisely those who strive for rightness out of love and yet err? When we do something wrong, we should call our action wrong; but when we act out of love, we should realize we are good. Giving credit where credit is due is, after all, a step in the right direction.

STUDY QUESTIONS

If we agree that the call to be a Christian is the call to grow, what does the call to grow look like?

How would you define the conscience?

Are you able to distinguish superego from conscience? Give an example of when you confused the conscience with the superego?

Over the past year, what lessons in life did you learn that helped you to form your conscience?

Explain whether you would call a person good who strives for the right out of love but fails.

Chapter Three

SIN

Through a series of steps I want to wear down some long-standing presuppositions that we have about sin. Then I want to propose a new notion of sin.

When I was about seven years old, like other Brooklyn Catholics, I already knew a great deal about my faith. We studied the Baltimore catechism and were tested weekly. We had May crownings, the Feast of All Saints when we dressed as our namesakes, first communions, confirmations, and Friday benedictions (where, along with "Tantum Ergo," we sang "An Army of Youth"). My mother was in the Rosary Altar Society, my father was in the Knights of Columbus, and I was an altar boy. We knew Latin, understood what a maniple was, and kept a sacrament of the sick kit at home. We were Roman Catholic.

While most of the time being a Roman Catholic was an uplifting experience, it was when sin and confession were introduced into our lives that we came into contact with what philosophers call "existential anxiety." Probably the greatest anxiety circled around making a good confession or, rather, failing to make one.

I remember walking to school with a seven-year-old classmate considering the case of someone who forgets to tell all their sins in one particular confession and then the next time goes to confession and forgets to tell those sins yet again and how all the subsequent confessions would be bad just as the first one was. I feared it happening to me. I remarked to my friend, "And how could I ever remember to redo all those confessions?" Then, just as we were about to cross the street, in the middle of my angst-ridden monologue, my friend shared with me his ultimate fear: "Just imagine being hit by a car and not being in the state of grace!"

Catholic life in the late 1950s had a certain give and take. You always felt the give, but you also felt the take, and sin and hell were the takes. We worried about sin and confession a lot.

At one point I learned what a mortal sin was and how we commit it. It needed to be a grave act, committed with full knowledge and full consent of the will. These seemed to me to be significant conditions. After one Sunday mass I was walking home with my grandmother when I asked, "Grandma, I've been thinking about mortal sin. Who could ever do something really big and wrong, really mean it, and really want to do it? It just seems awfully hard to do all three." "You're right, Jimmy. It's very hard to commit a mortal sin." No more consoling words could have been spoken.

Not surprisingly, years later I became a moral theologian. In my years of study, I found a text that contradicted my grandmother. It was in Thomas Aquinas's *Summa Theologiae*. He asked whether St. Peter sinned mortally when he denied Christ. Thomas's answer was remarkable. But before reading his answer, consider what your answer to the question might be: grave matter, full knowledge, and full consent. Did Peter sin mortally? He was denying Christ. That was definitely grave matter. Did he have full knowledge, however? With a lot of anxiety pumping through Peter, could he fully understand what he was really being asked? Did he have the presence of mind to recognize the gravity of his sin? Furthermore, could he possibly have had full consent? Certainly, he did not want to be in that situation; he did not want to deny Jesus. Could we ever call his consent "full"? Without full knowledge and full consent, could Peter have sinned mortally?

Yes, says Thomas. Peter's denial was a mortal sin. He could have said he was Jesus's friend. He did not; therefore, Thomas argues, he had full knowledge and full consent. Thomas saw full consent and full knowledge not as separate conditions but rather as parts of the entire composite scene. Thomas did not use these conditions to exonerate as we do today; he used them to illustrate that the sin was mortal. In other words, he interpreted full knowledge and full consent differently than we do, not looking for what was missing but rather recognizing what was there: Peter knew otherwise and could have acted otherwise; therefore there was knowledge and consent.

Thomas was a positive realist when it came to the human condition. He believed that we are capable, intelligent, and free and therefore competent with our moral lives. He also held that we often act without responsibility for our lives and actions. For this reason, he believed we frequently sinned mortally.

So how do we arbitrate my grandmother's insight that we hardly ever sin mortally with Thomas's that we frequently sin mortally? As much as I hate to say it, Thomas is basically right; my consoling grandmother was, like so many, a bit indulgent.

Perhaps the word *mortal* is a bit daunting when speaking of degrees of sin, but I think anyone who looks at the history of the way we have talked about sin would see that we have become an incredibly self-excusing people of God. We have managed to move from the assumption that generally, when we act, we act with knowledge and consent, to the present habit of acquitting one another from culpability by claiming lack of knowledge and consent.

Anyone who has done any therapy, for instance, knows the importance of claiming responsibility for one's actions. It is not morally, spiritually, or psychologically healthy to relinquish our competency. (Let me note, here, that I have not yet talked about what I mean by sin, but my first point is to rescue human freedom and responsibility from the present tendency to acquit too readily.)

How Bad Are We?

I believe one reason why we so frequently acquit is because we do not want to face how morally bad we actually are. Like most medieval theologians, Thomas believed that we frequently fail to exercise our moral responsibilities and that therefore most of us are going to hell. The medieval phrase that captured this belief was *massa damnata*, the "damned masses." Thomas did not invent this unhappy phrase. Augustine created it eight hundred years earlier, and, in fact, from the fourth to the twentieth century many, many church members believed it.

For some reason, somewhere around the 1960s, just as I was walking with my grandmother in Brooklyn, we began talking about God's universal offer of salvation and mercy, and we began doubting the phrase *massa damnata*. In the scriptures we began finding explicit and implicit assurances of the universal offer of salvation. Maybe we were sinners, but God was merciful toward all who called on him.

A generation after that we adapted our beliefs yet again. We began seeing that not only was God's merciful offer of salvation for all, but we also started to claim that God's creation was good and that because humanity was in God's image, we were especially good.

These assertions are true, certainly, but the biblical affirmation of our goodness as created in God's image is very different from the claim that in living out our lives we are morally good. Nonetheless, we went from the first goodness to the second with considerable ease and replaced the *massa damnata* with the *massa bona*. With uncommon frequency, in the 1970s, 1980s, and 1990s, we heard people preaching how good we are, how we all are surely going to enter God's kingdom, and so on. That is, rather than reminding ourselves we were sinners, but saved, we simply declared that we were good.

Curiously, many, many people stopped going to the sacrament of confession. Seventeen hundred years of sermons warning us that we could be among the majority of people going to hell was certainly an incentive for at least trying to be among the lucky minority. Now, after thirty years of sermons contradicting the earlier claims, we no longer feel the intimidation that prompted our frequent entries into the confessional box. Moreover, by insisting that we are so good, we are left with the inevitable question: If we are so good then why do we need confession?

Of course, we need to pause. Were theologians and preachers actually wrong for seventeen centuries in their presupposition regarding the *massa damnata*? I think they were as wrong as those who argue the contrary today. I think knowing the state of ourselves on Judgment Day is not in the purview of human estimation. Since in Matthew 25 all the sheep and all the goats had no idea of how their judgment day would be, I see no reason for despair or presumption about how our Judgment Day is going to turn out. It eludes us, and rightly so. In short, I think we need to tone down whatever "certainty" we have on either claim.

In a manner of speaking, previous generations recognized our sinfulness but failed to see the gift of grace, mercy, and salvation. The masses may have been sinful, but whether they were damned is another question. The dying words of Christ—"forgive them for they know not what they do" (Luke 23:24)—were not uttered solely for those standing on Golgotha. They have everlasting significance. We may not be the *massa damnata*, but we are evidently not the *massa bona* either. We are the sinful masses, saved. In a word, we are sinners, but loved.[1]

SINNING OUT OF OUR STRENGTH

I want to pose another question: Do we really sin out of our strength or out of our weakness? As one who hears confessions, I am always struck by how people confess their weaknesses repeatedly. Wherever we are weak, we confess it: I lost my temper; I failed to stand up to my boss; I drank too much. . . . We confess where we are weak.

Not only that, we actually spend quite a bit of moral effort striving to overcome or subdue the particular weakness. We confess: I struggle with my anger; I struggle with my lack of courage; I struggle with my drinking. Most of us expend most of our moral energy on our weaknesses. Predictably, at some point we fall short of our goals. And at that point we think we sin, and we confess yet again where our weakness is, where we failed, where we did something wrong.[2]

Of course, the area in our life where many of us are most complicated is in our sexuality. And, not surprisingly, where we have all sorts of weaknesses, we are constantly confessing. Where you and I are weak, messy, and broken, we believe we sin. In those same areas we expend great moral effort and yet we name that part of our lives as our sinfulness. Where we are weak, we sin. Or so we think.

Let me be clear. I think that when we suffer from moral weaknesses and do not try to overcome them, *then* we sin. But my experience tells me that many people are very attentive to their weaknesses and actually try to keep them in check, but they still fail. Are they sinning if they try as much as they can?

I think that focusing on our weaknesses allows us to avoid the real understanding of sin. By focusing on our weaknesses, we focus on the areas of our life where we feel impoverished and where we really believe that we are not as strong as it may seem. By focusing on our weaknesses, we inevitably believe that we are weak—good, but weak. If only I was stronger, we think. But do we really, primarily, sin out of our weakness? I do not think so.

As the medieval theologians understood well, every narrative in the Gospel is not about sinners sinning out of their weaknesses, but out of their strengths. When the publican and Pharisee are praying in the temple, the sin of the Pharisee is in his strength (Luke 18:9–14). He specifically considers what he has. When the rich man steps over Lazarus and ignores Lazarus at the gate and in need, the rich man's sin is not in his weakness, but in his strength (Luke 16:19–31). He could have done something; he did not—he sinned, precisely out of his strength. The steward who asked forgiveness for his debt is forgiven, but he's punished because he does not forgive the minor debt by his own employee. Out of his strength, the steward is convicted (Matt. 18:21–35). Think of the parable of the Good Samaritan—where is the sin? Even the robbers who committed the crime of beating the poor man on the road to Jericho are ignored. The focus is on the Levite and the priest; they could have acted, but they did not (Luke 10:25–37). They sinned precisely out of their strength. Or think of the Last Judgment. Note how the sheep and goats are separated—by what they could have done and whether they did it (Matt. 25:31–46).

Is it not odd, then, that the entire Gospel tradition has us sinning out of our strengths, and yet we think that we sin out of our weaknesses. But notice too that we have the same problem here as we did with my consoling grandmother: a certain self-understanding where we tend to think of ourselves as weak, as without knowledge, without freedom, without consent, whenever we consider ourselves as sinners. Why is that? Why do we think of ourselves as weak when we think of ourselves as sinners?

I think it is a fairly natural instinct, but I think it is profoundly self-deceptive. Not surprising, right? Is not the nature of sin to be self-deceptive, and would not our instinct be to deceive ourselves about the nature of our sinfulness? Because of this, we need to keep our eyes on the scriptures, because they help us be aware of at least two truths: that we are probably greater sinners than we admit and that we sin out of our strength.

SURPRISED BY SIN

But let us look to the scriptures again. How well do people know of their sinfulness? In the Gospel stories people are surprised to find out how sinful they are. This is extraordinary. Think for instance of the Last Judgment again. The goats ask, "But when did we not feed you? When did we not visit you?" They are clueless about their self-understanding as sinners. Similarly, the rich man is ignorant of his impending fate. He did not know he'd go to hell for not caring for Lazarus. Listen to him: "Father Abraham, tell my brothers," he pleads from Hades. Or what about the priest and the Levite who pass the wounded man in the Good Samaritan parable? Do they see what we see, that they have failed to be neighbors? Do we see anywhere within the parable someone stopping them and telling them, "Hmm, you two better realize that you just sinned by passing by the wounded man on the road"? Or again, the Pharisee with the publican. Does the Pharisee know the judgment of arrogance being attributed to him in his prayer? I'm always surprised at how dense the scriptural characters are about the state of their souls: they do not recognize their sinfulness. So why do we think that we recognize our sinfulness?

Domesticating and Trivializing Sin

Not only do we think we know our sinfulness, but we actually try to put sin into nice, discreet, manageable categories: we can confess our sin, its kind, and its number. In little packages, we tidily wrap up our sins and present them for confession. John Mahoney in *The Making of Moral Theology* studies our tradition of confessing sins and argues that we have "domesticated" our sinfulness.[3]

"I got angry at my spouse three times, I lied once, I wasn't honest on my taxes, I missed mass on Sunday, I committed adultery once." Let us just stop and think about that anger for a moment. Just one of the times . . . let us try to take it in. What was it about, how long did it last, how many people did we exclude in order to demonstrate our anger, who was affected, how much, to what extent? Let us do a meditation on each of these sins that we so nicely named, categorized, numbered, and confessed.

After that meditation, let us ask ourselves whether we even scratched the surface of our sinfulness. The nature of sin in the Gospel is, after all, pervasive, deceptive, and elusive. Have we learned that? Have we not seen constantly in the Gospels how hard it is to know of one's sinfulness, let alone how impossible it is to subdue sin and then to name it and present it according to kind and number?

We have domesticated sin, and in domesticating sin we have trivialized it, as Mahoney notes. We tuck sin into nice prepackaged categories. But in order to trivialize sin, we need the evident ones, the ones on the surface, the obvious ones or the easy-to-name ones. So we say, "I got angry three times."

Our weak sins are also the ones that we really work hard at. These sins do not highlight our coldness of heart, our mean-spiritedness, our pettiness, our deep-seated resentfulness, our sinfulness. When we name our "weak" sins, we claim simultaneously that we struggled, that we sincerely made an effort, that we were, after all, vulnerable and excusable.

But we have deep within us some incredible, hidden sinfulness. Albert Camus recognized our secret sinfulness in his great work *The Plague*.[4] Telling the story of a people suddenly infected by a plague, Camus conveys the greatness and the smallness of the people of the great city of Oran who respond gracefully and wickedly to the crisis. But as suddenly as the plague came, equally suddenly it recedes. The people who were once completely unaware of how deeply vulnerable they were to a plague learn during the epidemic how foolish they were. When the plague disappears at the end, the people breathe a sigh of relief. All the plague has done is recede into hiding; the citizens think that they are safe, that they have subdued it, but they have not. And they have forgotten how vulnerable they are.

Of course, the plague was a metaphor. For Camus, the real plague was the deep-rooted selfishness of people that showed itself so manifestly throughout World War II. During the war, while a few were heroic, many simply avoided their neighbor; they avoided responding to their neighbor in need. Instead, they collaborated and protected only themselves. As in the plague, in the war people showed how they really only think of themselves.

We should look at this from another angle. In my introductory course on moral theology I have my students read a brilliant article titled "Autobiography and Self-deception," by David Burrell and Stanley Hauerwas.[5] The authors examine the life of Albert Speer, a promising architect, who sought acceptance, whose talent was recognized by Adolf Hitler, and who was eventually brought by Hitler into his own entourage. Hitler commissioned Speer to be the architect of Nuremburg and Berlin.

Speer was a "nice" man, a family man. He had none of the incredibly vicious, hate-driven obsessions that many leaders of the Third Reich (like Goebbels, Goering, and Himmler) possessed. He was basically a man interested in his architectural work, his career, and his family. He also was attracted to fame.

He was incredibly efficient. His efficiency assisted the Reich considerably when he was made minister of armaments in 1943. Then he developed a way to get munitions to the front lines of the somewhat-collapsing Nazi forces and thus protracted the war by nearly two years. It was not the treacherous thugs and the bigots who empowered the Nazis during the last years of their disgusting war—it was someone who did not share their ideology, someone who had no ideology, someone who did not hate. He loved, but only himself and his family, and certainly not the stranger or the marginalized. He did not bother to love. He was simply someone who was efficient, who did the work well because he enjoyed having Hitler's confidence and architectural commissions. He traded his efficiency for fame, recognition, and contracts. He was a modern-day Faust.

Burrell and Hauerwas suggest that when we think of sinning we should think of Speer rather than Hitler or one of his gang, because chances are that we are more capable of becoming a Speer than a Hitler. Sure, Hitler sins, and he sins in remarkable ways, but the sin of Speer is more ordinary, more familiar, more likely. It fits in with that haunting insight of Hannah Arendt about the "banality of evil." Give us the right place, the right time, the right conditions, and it may not take us much to become a Speer. We are all subject to the plague, no?

The sin of Speer is not in what he did, but in what he did not do. He did not murder, torture, or rape; he did not even hate or inflame passions. For Speer conveyed himself to others in such a way that his subordinates did not even approach him with news of Nazi atrocities. Besides being efficient and seeking Hitler's approval, the only other activity Speer tried was not knowing what the Nazis were doing. He would not want his life or his family's disturbed. In a word, he simply did not bother himself with news of the monstrosities that the Nazis were performing. And as minister of armaments this was not easy avoidance, for he was directly responsible for the horrible "labor" camps.

I want to suggest that, as a matter of fact, the real reason why we are more likely to become a Speer than a Hitler is because, like Speer, we do not want to see our sinfulness, we are presumptuous about our goodness, and we do not think we are wicked. In fact, like Speer, we think of ourselves as different from those, like Hitler, who hate. We think when we sin we are weak, and we deliberately underestimate what we could have done.

But where is sin, then? How can we name it so as to appreciate how pervasive and deceptive it is? How can we recognize its strength in our strength and its affinity to our own hidden humanity?

Sin as the Failure to Bother to Love

To capture the breadth, depth, and pervasiveness of sin, I propose that sin is simply the failure to bother to love. That is it. This definition of sin is a biblical one: it captures the sin of Matthew's goats, Lazarus's rich man, the wounded man's priest and the Levite, the publican's Pharisee, and so on. Each of the Bible stories that refers us to sin refers us to what one could have done and did not do. Not only the stories that we have looked at, but others as well: the man who did not invest the talent (Matt. 25:14–30), the virgins who were not vigilant (Matt. 25:1–13), the son who did not go into the field to work as he said he would (Matt. 21:28–32). Sin is in the failure to bother to love.

Our sin is usually not in what we did, not in what we could not avoid, not in what we tried not to do. Our sin is usually where you and I are comfortable, where we do not feel the need to bother—where, like the Pharisee, or even Speer, we have found complacency, a complacency not where we rest in being loved but where we rest in our delusional self-understanding of how much better we are than others. It is at that point of self-satisfaction that—like Speer, the Pharisee, the prodigal's older brother, or the rich man—we usually do not bother to love.

Let us look at this notion of sin as a failure to bother to know from another point of view. While teaching at Fordham University, I lived in the dorms with the undergraduates. For several years, I lived with sophomores. These people were now familiar with the lay of the land, had gotten over homesickness, and were pursuing their own adult identities. They were a lot of fun. I particularly enjoyed noticing how they talked about their parents. In the beginning of the year, the students often described their parents as Joe and Jackie Cool, in part to win the interest of new friends. But as acquaintances and friendships developed, they started talking about the ways that their parents missed the mark. In a way, they made their parents their competitors: they were not going to make their parents' same mistakes.

They divided their parents' mistakes into two categories. First, there was the "my-mom-and-dad-can-be-a-pair-of-klutzes." These were harmless but humorous accounts that usually centered on simple accidents or mistakes: Mom making a wrong turn or Dad forgetting something important. Of course, they were greatly embellished and sometimes complete fabrications. But through them, these nineteen-year-olds could feel slightly superior to their absent (and undefended) parents.

The other descriptions of parental mistakes were not humorous, nor were they disclosed as publicly. These were rather confidential disclosures between roommates, friends, or lovers. They were painful private accounts—probably a lot truer than the comic public ones—about how shortcomings in one parent affected the life of this particular daughter or son. They were tales of a parent who drank too much, who worked hard but flew off the handle in anger, or who was too timid to communicate adequately with spouse, employer, or child. In any event, these were long-running accounts of how a particular parent's own shortcomings hurt this particular child.

Curiously, the students soon began evaluating these mistakes. They dismissed the first set as simple error. But they eventually wanted to know whether the harm caused by the second set meant that their parent did not love them. They wanted to figure out whether they meant anything to the overworked, underconfident, obsessive parent. Assuredly their parent was wrong for drinking too much, blowing a fuse, or hiding out, but was that wrongness a sign that the parent did not love? Curiously, they probably did their best moral reasoning as they wrestled with this key question.

Eventually, they were able to see that there was a distinct possibility that the parent may actually have been trying so hard at being a good parent precisely when the personal problems erupted. Appreciating their parent as limited and recognizing their parent as capable of causing considerable harm at times, they still saw that the parent may well have been trying to overcome the timidity, wrestle with the demon, or tame the anger, and, despite the attempts, still failed. In fact, they could go so far as to recognize in the parent's attempt to resist the weakness, the desire of the parent to be as loving as possible. The parent was wrong, but not because she did not bother to love.

This insight was often matched by the student, long silent, with neither the comic nor sad stories of parental shortcomings. That student could remark that for him nothing went wrong, childhood had no crisis, and the parent was neither a klutz nor dysfunctional. As a matter of fact, he was given a good deal, or so he thought. But now, listening to the struggles of his friends' parents, he was not sure that his own parents ever loved him, ever bothered with him. Could life have been so routinely facile that the parents never bothered to love? The moment that this fear was raised, the students knew that they were facing something terribly profound about human life. For not only were they faced with a peer who was uncertain about his parents' love, but they were also glimpsing that key insight that we saw in the last chapter: we can never simply presume from right or wrong activity that one is good or bad, loving or not.

If we want to know what sin is, these students' insights are terribly instructive. Who is the sinner in these narratives? The parents who tried to be caring, responsible, and loving, yet caused harm, or those who did well but loved little? Clearly, I think sin is more in the latter than in the former. This is, after all, the point we arrived at in the last chapter.

LEARNING TO CONFESS OUR SINFULNESS

We saw in the last chapter that a good conscience—that is, a conscience that strives for the right—does not guarantee that the action will in fact be right. Therein is the distinction in moral theology between goodness and rightness.

Now we are looking through another perspective at the same distinction, here as it relates to badness and wrongness. All our weaknesses, all our failings are clearly instances of our wrongness, where you and I fall short of the mark—where we hurt others, even when we try not to. But we've been trying to get to sin, which is badness, not wrongness.

If the real moral measure of our lives is moral goodness—that is, where we love, where we strive for the right—then sin is its opposite—where we are bad, where we fail to bother to love. Just as it is difficult to know where there is goodness, similarly it is hard to know where there is sin. Sin is, as it is in the parents of the sophomore, in coldness of heart. And it takes a while to find where the heart is cold.

But that coldness is what we find in all the Gospel stories that speak of sin: the goats, the rich man, the priest, the Levite, the Pharisee, the virgins, even the older unforgiving brother of the prodigal—all of them are basically thoughtless and coldhearted. But they are also, as we've seen, blind to their coldheartedness, to their wickedness, to their sinfulness. Their blindness is rather remarkable.

Think for a moment of the complacency of the older brother of the parable of the prodigal son: he does not see any wrongdoing that he's done. His brother's wrongdoing is not his. His brother has broken the law; he has not. Not seeing any wrongdoing of his own, he acquits himself of any badness. He believes that his brother does not deserve the celebration; on the contrary, in all his pettiness the older brother thinks he deserves the celebration. The Pharisee does the same thing: he sees the publican and the publican's wrongdoing. In that light he sees that he has done no wrong, and, like the prodigal's older brother, he acquits himself of badness. None of these see their own coldheartedness, these hearts that fail to bother to love: not the priest, nor the Levite, nor the goats.

We are a little different. We obsess about our wrongdoing and fret about our weakness and confess our vulnerability. Where we struggle over our wrongdoing, we name it as sin. But is not sin in fact where we do not struggle, where we do not bother to love? Sin is not in our weakness; it is in our strength. It is where, like the older brother, we are complacent—not in the sense that we rest in being loved, but that we believe we have measured up, that we are just fine, that, like all the other New Testament sinners, we are satisfied with ourselves.

If sin is very deceptive, if sin is hidden, if it is not where we have evident weakness but where we are strong, how can we confess it? At least we can name our wrongdoing. How do we name our failure to bother to love?

The late German moral theologian Franz Böckle talks about the effectiveness of confession. What he means is, if we do not confess our sinfulness, we never recognize our sinfulness. But, if we acknowledge our moral faults, we discover the depths of our faults. In fact, as we confess, we learn more and more about our sinfulness.[6]

I find it helpful here to consider times when we have had a very unfortunate argument with a loved one. Afterward, as we revisit the dispute, estranged from our loved one, we live in our own heads where we keep playing tapes about the other being at fault, about our being innocent and their being responsible to seek reconciliation. If the moment of reconciliation ever begins, if we ever start talking to the other, however, we often find ourselves readily admitting that, as a matter of fact, we may have erred; it may have been our fault too. In other words, when we begin speaking with a willingness to acknowledge our own faults, our tapes change and we become more able to recognize the situation for what it was.

Böckle then suggests that when you and I begin to recognize our sinfulness, Christ's light often shines on us to let us see how much we have sinned and to see how we could have loved. Until we begin to recognize our sinfulness, we really cannot understand it. This is, of course, Ignatius's insight for the first week of the *Spiritual Exercises.* There, in the light of God's merciful love, we learn how we are sinners but saved.

I think that the confession of sin, however, is not an itemized list. Certainly there may be some wrong actions that were sinful that were evident absences of love. But we must be careful that, in naming our wrong actions, we do not deceive ourselves into thinking that we have subdued and domesticated our sinfulness, that we have recognized our badness, that we have captured the pervasiveness of where we have not loved.[7] I think real confession, tasting the real fruit of the sacrament of reconciliation, is found when we try to name not only the wrong we have done but also the ways we have not loved. There we encounter a simple resigned sense that we are quite capable of being much more loving persons than we are. It is an encounter with our extraordinary propensity to arrogance, self-sufficiency, and moral narcissism. It is where we come into contact with our badness, our self-complacency. But, interestingly, we can only do it with the love of Christ; his mercy lets us see it.

Social Sin

This definition of sin as the failure to bother to love takes a lot of individualism out of sin, because it highlights the call to love and therefore acknowledges the many ways that we are all related.

This notion of sin then is compatible with social sin. In fact, this notion of sin gives those who support the concept of social sin an even greater claim on us, simply because such a notion of sin would have to be inevitably social: If sin is the failure to bother to love, what sin would not be social?

All sin is social. Wherever people are suffering, we need to ask ourselves, are we adequately attuned to their needs? But that question leads us to another question. If sin is pervasive and deceptive, then we cannot simply ask ourselves whether we are adequately attuned to their needs, because inevitably there will be something in our society that will keep us from knowing about the needs of those for whom we are responsible. This is, of course, how Hauerwas's Albert Speer, Camus's France, and Matthew's goats managed not to sense the call to love those who were near them: society provided them with blinders from recognizing what they needed to know. And we can be as sure that our societies, just as my grandmother did, routinely acquit us from the moral responsibility for the way we live and the effects our lives have on others. We live in societies that do not want us to be disturbed.

In his "Letter from a Birmingham Jail," Martin Luther King Jr. wrote not to outright racists; rather, he wrote to white preachers (not unlike Albert Speer) who should have known better about the Gospel call to love and mercy, but who instead became complacent with a white racist society. King asks, why were they so comfortable when the Gospel was so clear? He recognizes that the societies we live in anesthetize us from the conscience that prompts us to ask, do we bother to love?[8]

As a boy living where I did in Brooklyn and later living on eastern Long Island, I never thought of racism. I never thought that there were any barriers for black people. As a boy, I never knew black people and while I thought (and heard) that people in the south were racists, I never thought we were. My society isolated me from thinking that maybe I was a participant in a strategy that was actually exclusive and deeply racist.

How would I learn to think otherwise? I learned to listen to some of my teachers, especially the nuns. They helped me, hard as it was, to learn to ask questions and to think outside the box, to realize that life was more complicated than I thought and that some people really were victims of some pernicious, but unspoken policies. They invited me to assume another perspective.

When I began to understand my society and my neighborhood better, I began to see how I fit comfortably into a pattern of benefits and goods that were excluded from others. From there I began to appreciate that it is not until we begin to see the other side that we begin to understand our own much better.

Years later, after entering the Jesuits, I was given a lot more opportunities to learn more and more about life. During my second summer in the novitiate I had a job to locate all the migrant camps in a nice, family-values county in upstate New York. Working with another Jesuit, we drove more than one hundred miles a day to find one camp after another. The incredible hardships of these people were literally hidden from the "good" Christians of the town. Yet the town prospered because of the work of these poor people. Farmers could not have profited without the cheap labor of these nearly enslaved migrant workers. I remember listening to the workers' stories, about their debts to their bosses, about their lack of ownership of any tangible goods, about their constant movements from New York to Florida and back, following crop seasons but always involved in backbreaking work. How would they ever get out of this cycle of poverty? They were trapped.

Later I would see the same set of divisions, where people were trapped on the other side, whether in tenements in New York or garbage heaps in Manila. People were literally stuck in their situation and the structures of society wanted them to be there. But rarely did people on the other side of the division see how profoundly unjust and dehumanizing these structures were.

Years ago, in 1932, an American theologian Reinhold Niebuhr wrote about this phenomenon in *Moral Man, Immoral Society*. He argued that individuals can be motivated by a sense of compassion and justice, but that societies are not capable of such transcendence. On the contrary, societies resist understanding their hypocrisy, their oppressive structures, and their need for reform. In fact, they promote, through a variety of forums, a complacency in their members, subtly coaxing people from seeing the world in which we actually live.

Movies love to look at this disturbing reality. In the *Truman Show*, Jim Carrey plays a character locked into a TV show by media manipulation, thoroughly unaware that reality is beyond the stage set. In *Pleasantville*, Joan Allen, Tobey Maguire, and Jeff Daniels play people trapped in a 1950s-like society that has no diversity, no emotional life, and no color. What they cannot see, they cannot understand. In *Far from Heaven*, Dennis Quaid, Julianne Moore, and Dennis Haysbert live in the 1950s society, which prided itself on moral standards that kept them from facing the oft-hidden issues of race, love, and sexuality. In *The Island*, Ewan McGregor and Scarlett Johansson live in a near-perfect society of order and control, dreaming of winning the lottery that includes a trip to the island. But these dreamers do not know that they are merely clones whose body parts will be harvested when they win the lottery. From *Total Recall* to the *Thirteenth Floor*, movie directors invite us to see that the context in which we find ourselves might be controlling us from seeing reality as it actually is.

Often enough our society feeds off of others, and we are oblivious to the harms and injustices that it perpetrates. Still, we need to ask ourselves, are we responsible for this? Are we responsible for the fact that the world cannot support the lifestyle which most Americans live: the energy resources, the meat and fish consumption, the use of transportation, and so on?

Thomas Aquinas would simply say, could we have known otherwise? In each of the movies I mentioned, the heroes are those who find out the truth against all odds. They allow themselves to think outside the box and to wonder whether they really understand what is actually going on. We are required to do the same. And our failure to learn otherwise is a clear indication how we sin from strength, from a failure to bother to love. In the comfort and luxury of our society, we keep one another from knowing what we need to know, what we could know, and what we do not bother to learn.

Faced with this notion of sin, should we not despair? Should we not give up? Should we just go away sad?

There is that famous parable of the rich young man. In it, he goes up to Jesus and asks what he must do to get into heaven, and Jesus tells him to observe the commandments. The rich young man responds complacently: I did all that. But Jesus says, okay, give up everything and come follow me. And the rich man goes away sad.

When we think that God wants us to love as best we can, inevitably we become like the rich young man, very unwilling to love more than what is comfortable. When we are really honest, at some point we see that we are each the rich young man. None of us could do anything more than the rich young man.[9] We eventually do not bother to love.

What are we to do? That is, of course, the question the disciples ask Jesus when the young man walks away. Then Jesus explains that what is impossible for us is possible for God. Even though the rich young man could not win his salvation, God in Jesus Christ could.

And that is what sin teaches us. When, like the rich man, we get a glimpse of our sinfulness, we have a choice—to go away despairing or to become modest, humble, and grateful for Christ's salvation.

When we choose the latter, when we really get a glimpse of what we could do but do not bother to, we no longer look on the other as worse than we are. We no longer nestle into our complacency; we become instead transformed in humility.

Furthermore, when we see our sinfulness through the salvation won by Christ, we do not become paralyzed by guilt. Rather we become freed from it, but by Christ. And we never dare look back at our sinfulness lest we become like Lot's wife, paralyzed by our own histories of failing to bother to love.

Sin teaches us never to look back complacently but always to look forward in love and in hope. It teaches us that indeed we are strong and capable of much and that much of our history is filled with how we could have loved but did not bother to love. But the history of sin is one that rebukes us into remembering that we do indeed need our Redeemer and Savior. In short, because of sin, we need Christ. Without that knowledge, we fail to recognize that need.

When we recognize that, we recognize also our neighbor, particularly the alienated and marginalized, those who are overwhelmed by the social structures that harness them but benefit us. And we begin to realize that until we work in solidarity and justice for all, we have not yet accepted the liberating redemption of Jesus Christ.

Grace is not cheap. When we finally understand what it is that Christ has done for us, we inevitably learn to open our eyes and see what we can do. And from that strength, we learn what we need to know and need to do.

STUDY QUESTIONS

How do you define sin? What is for you a good example of sin?

Why is it important to understand not only that we are called to love, but that we sin? Do you think people are willing to see that they are sinners? Do you think we should just see ourselves as good?

Do you think we primarily sin from strength or weakness? Why is it that so many people think that we sin from weakness?

What movies can you think of that try to show us that we are indeed living in a self-deceptive world?

Are you hope-filled that we can work for a more just world?

Chapter Four

SUFFERING

W HEN WE EXAMINE SUFFERING, WE NEED TO RECOGNIZE TWO very different types of discussions on this topic. The more familiar occurs in academic gatherings, which produce many philosophical and theological works about suffering and its "meaning." The less familiar occurs in those intimate settings in which we are called to respond to someone who is suffering and who wants to talk with us about her or his suffering; in that setting, we usually listen rather than talk.

In the academic context there is less interest in the actual sufferer and more interest in the question of theodicy—that is, how can we reconcile a merciful, providential God with suffering. These academic works are really not addressed to sufferers, but rather to a general audience philosophically or theologically interested in the questions that result from the reality of suffering in a world created by a loving God. These works tend to be theoretical and speculative, rather than practical and concrete.

Another way of describing these two conversations is to note that there is the intellectual level, where we "search for reasons *why* there is suffering in the world and *why* it comes to some and not to others." The other is much less abstract and much more strategic, what some call the survival level, where we "provide support and comfort to the person who is experiencing suffering."[1]

In the latter case, we listen to how the suffering person tries to figure out ways of surviving through their suffering.

As you have probably guessed by now, I am more interested in understanding suffering from the viewpoint of the sufferer. Then we can turn to the question of suffering and its meaning. In all this, we need to learn what our response to suffering ought to be.

Voice

Faced with suffering, we need to recognize the critical importance of listening. In order to appreciate the importance of listening, however, we must appreciate the importance of the sufferer's voice.

Nowhere has the relationship between the voice and suffering been better captured than by Elaine Scarry. In the first chapter of her book, *The Body in Pain*, Scarry studies the relationship between voice and torture. She explains that the object of torture is not to learn information, but rather to force the tortured person to accuse herself and thereby to recognize the torturer's power. Torturers derive their understanding of power from the voices of the tortured. Thus the torturer aims to make tortured persons convict themselves. This happens when the tortured person's body is so broken with pain that she is unable to keep her voice from submitting to the fictive power of the torturer. The aim of torture, then, is to tear the voice from its body, to make the tortured person capitulate to the torturer's authority. Scarry writes, "The goal of the torturer is to make the one, the body, emphatically and crushingly *present* by destroying it, and to make the other, the voice, *absent* by destroying it." At the end of torture, the tortured person is finally left voiceless; once the voice in agony acknowledges the torturer's power, it falls into shameful, isolating silence.[2]

Scarry notes that the tortured person's most difficult wound to heal is also the voice. For this reason, Amnesty International assists the tortured, unable out of shame to tell their narratives, to read and understand their records so that one day they may articulate or give

68

voice to the truth of the atrocities they endured. When they are able to finally speak the truth about the experience of torture, they enter on to the journey of healing, but until they do, they live in silent shame. Scarry's work convincingly demonstrates the centrality of the human voice in attaining healing integration.

Through the voice we express our fundamental concerns, maintain relationships, organize our world, and locate ourselves among others. But when we suffer, our dependence on the voice is itself troublesome particularly because the terrors and trauma associated with the threat and the loss experienced in suffering often inhibit the sufferer from intelligibly articulating the cause and/or depth of suffering. Moreover, the voice itself, not merely the sufferer's intelligence, is also, especially in times of pain, muted. Thus, when the voice is unable to express itself, the sufferer loses the most integral way by which a sufferer can communicate and remain in contact with the community that supports her. Progressively, studies show us not only the therapeutic function that the voice has in the life of the sufferer, but conversely the compounded suffering that occurs when the voice is ignored, lost, or silenced. For, like torture itself, the act of silencing a sufferer, or worse, of making a suffering person speak against herself, is a violent action.

Here I think of not only the tortured but also of the sick, and I think of the many instances when we try to keep those who are sick from telling us how badly they feel. We think in our exercises that we are encouraging the sick to look on the so-called brighter side, when actually we are only telling the patient, "Don't, please don't tell me what you're worrying about. I can't bear to hear it." Of course, the sufferer is the one who has to bear the reality that we only refuse to hear.

I think particularly of those patients—who, facing their own mortality, find that same violence in the habitual acts wherein physicians and nurses as well as family and friends ignore, silence, translate, or belittle the voices of patients. How many times, when a person's death is near, the only one disposed to speaking about the future is the patient, but the discomfort of the others is so great as to inhibit, diminish, or worse, contradict the very person who wants to speak about her forthcoming death.

The sufferer's voice is their lifeline to the world from which they find themselves progressively isolated. Thus, through the voice, the one isolated in suffering is able to reach out to others. For this reason we need to consider not only the voice of the sufferer but also the listening of those who seek to respond to the sufferer.

Responding to the Sufferer by Listening

Listening is all the more important when the sufferer is not immediately forthcoming about her own well-being or about the strategies of her survival. This inability to express easily one's suffering or one's strategies is, in fact, a commonplace, since the act of articulating the perceived threat to one's world is itself traumatic.

In a source that I am unable to remember or locate, I read that in many patient interviews, patients do not name their major ailment until they first mention one or two lesser ones. That is, during an interview, the first two items reported by some patients are not the reasons for the patient's visit, but the third item is—"I haven't slept well. I have an occasional headache, but nothing serious. Oh yes, I have a lump on my breast." We delay the reporting because we have never had to face what we fear facing. Thus, on occasion, the inattentive or rushed physician sends home a patient who never utters the real reason for their concern. (Here is a curious parallel. In my training for hearing confessions, I was informed that it is not until the third sin that penitents express their serious sins. Not uncommonly we hear things like "I swore, I missed mass, I committed adultery, I was testy at work.") Listening requires an active patience, a soliciting ear.

Still, there is something more integral for responding to suffering than simply hearing the correct condition. The act of listening should welcome the sufferer who wants to speak. Allowing the sufferer to speak is a very biblical stance. Here I want us to consider God's listening to the suffering of Job and then the suffering of Jesus.

The book of Job begins with God delighting in his servant Job, an upright man. The devil says to God, if Job was visited with suffering, he wouldn't be all that wonderful. With that the story unfolds of calamitous actions happening to Job that lead to the loss of his wealth, the deaths of his children, and the covering of his body with pustules. Job wonders, *Why me?* He laments and cries out to God. He hears no answer from God, but is visited by his "friends." Surprisingly, they come and tell him that his suffering is due to his own fault. They claim, a person suffers after doing something wrong. Job is responsible, therefore, for his suffering, they surmise. Poor Job is not only suffering, but being blamed for it as well.

J. David Pleins asks, where is God in the midst of Job's suffering and complaint? Why does God not respond immediately to Job? Why does God let Job be judged and silenced by his so-called friends? Pleins responds that it is not God's absence but "God's silence [that] dominates the discussions of Job with his friends."[3] Pleins contends that God is the only one who gives Job a hearing, who allows Job to utter his complaint, and who gives Job the time to find a way of articulating his understanding of his situation. God is the one who, by listening, empowers Job's struggle and witnesses Job's integrity. God is the listener to Job. The others interrupt, confound, or silence Job.

This insight about a listening God is applicable to understanding the same "absence" or "silence" of God at Golgotha. We might wonder what those few witnesses thought when, as they stood helpless at the cross of Jesus, they heard Jesus's words, "My God, my God, why have you forsaken me?" (Matt. 27:46). But they listened to the cry of the suffering Jesus. Is God absent or, as Pleins suggests, is God listening? God witnesses to Jesus's agony and does not contend with Jesus's complaint, but gives Jesus a full hearing. God's silence both in Job and at the crucifixion conveys a God who listens actively, accompanying us in our suffering, allowing and empowering us to speak.

How many times have we acted differently? How many times have we said to one in their suffering, "Oh, don't say that!" "Oh, you don't mean that!" "Oh, but that's not right!" How many times do our standards of etiquette or decorum prompt us to interrupt the one who is lamenting her or his suffering? Against those times is the God of Job and Jesus listening to the cry of the sufferer.

This listening stands as an important witness to the sufferer and as a key alternative to another Christian urge, which is to interpret in the face of suffering. A senior colleague with whom I normally agree argues that Christians differentiate suffering from pain precisely in that "pain demands a response, while suffering demands an interpretation." I am not too sure that suffering demands an interpretation because so much suffering is so senseless. If suffering is so senseless, how could it have meaning?

In fact, I think the Christian urge to translate or interpret another's suffering can also be as violent as the act of silencing. I think here specifically of when Catholic leaders known for wanting to better Christian-Jewish relations let their own theology of suffering interpret the Jewish suffering in the Holocaust. Worse still is the insistence of Christians to speak about another's suffering, especially when they were the cause of that suffering. Marcel Sarot brings this point out poignantly in his "Auschwitz, Morality, and the Suffering of God."[4] There Sarot cites numerous instances of Christians translating or interpreting the meaning of Jewish questions and answers in the aftermath of Auschwitz. He especially addresses the Christian insistence to answer the Jewish sufferer who asks, "Where is God in all this?" Indeed, one has to remind the Christian that the Jew might not necessarily be looking for an answer to the question. Sarot calls his fellow Christian theologians to draw a moratorium on raising up Auschwitz as providing testimony necessary to understand faith and suffering, and he contends that the primary question that we Christians should raise in the face of Auschwitz is "How can we prevent that Christianity ever again can provide fertile soil for antisemitism and kindred movements?"

The Christian insistence on interpreting in the face of suffering should give way, I think, to the Jewish insistence on listening. One writer argues that "Christians would do better to face up to the pointlessness [of suffering], taking a lesson from the Hebrew scriptures. The psalms of lament . . . make no attempt to explain or palliate. Instead they give voice to human anguish, rage and despair on the apparent assumption that the God of Israel is strong enough to take it."[5]

Still, the call to listen to the voice of the one who is suffering is not always easy because sometimes the sufferer cannot speak. For instance, often suffering results precisely because a person is in pain and unable to express herself. In some instances this inability to speak is an even greater suffering than the pain itself because the sufferer is acutely aware of her isolation and is unable to communicate it. In particular, the person in chronic pain finds often that the pain perpetually keeps the sufferer from speaking. Pain inhibits the sufferer from doing the only thing that the sufferer wants to do: communicate her pain.

To assist the one suffering we need to remember the empathetic quality of pain that helps us acknowledge the depth of the other's suffering. Through empathy we can develop an aesthetic sense by which we can try to apprize the suffering of another who cannot speak but who communicates her suffering through a variety of movements. This aesthetic sense can be especially developed when the listener is attentive to the nature of suffering in her or his own life. When we become aware of the narrative of pain within our own bodies, we become familiar again with the desire to give voice to our own pain, hopefully assisting us to learn to listen to another's own "silent" narrative of suffering. Revisiting the terrain of one's own past suffering establishes the groundwork for becoming a compassionate and perceptive listener.

That the body can express the depth and complexity of suffering is very important. Where there is no voice to express the suffering, then we are reminded that "the body never lies." Thus, even when the sufferer cannot voice in any way her or his suffering, still the body may be able to communicate its suffering.

Here we can accompany another as we read aloud the psalms of lament as a means by which a listener can enter into solidarity with those who can only groan out or twist and turn in their suffering.[6] With these psalms, the sufferer, unable to express or name the particularity of her suffering, may be able to sense a welcoming acknowledgment by the listener of the desire to communicate to some extent the depth of personal suffering. By reciting the psalms for one unable to speak, we can become the sufferer's surrogate voice.

Still, there may be instances when the sufferer may not want to communicate, may not want yet to share her or his suffering. In fact, not talking might be for some a temporary survival strategy. Here I recall how my niece Megan responded to the awful news that she was out of remission. Because of her cancer she had lost a year of high school, just one year before graduation. In remission she returned to her high school a year later, but now with a different senior class. She made many friends in this new class and was quite happy. She learned about coming out of remission, however, about six weeks before her senior graduation.

The hospital staff wanted to talk about a bone marrow transplant. She informed them that there would be no transplant until she was graduated from high school. There had been enough conversations about the transplant earlier in her cancer, she maintained, and it was already known that her lone sibling was a match and had agreed to be the donor. A day after graduation she would be ready for the transplant, but there would be no discussion before then.

This was an awkward time. When she would come into Boston to treat the occasional infections that she developed during these six weeks, I would sit with her in the hospital. One day I said, "Megan, I don't want to discuss the transplant. I know you don't want any of us to. But could you give me an indication that you know what lays before you?" "I do know," she said.

She knew that she might not survive the transplant, but she also knew that she could celebrate her graduation. She had already lost one graduation due to her first year of treatments and she was not going to lose another graduation. Her graduation was wonderful!

Later, Megan underwent the transplant and all of its "opportunistic" infections. She bore those indignities with the same indomitable spirit as she had the earlier ones. Then, after passing the famed one-hundred-days-after-transplant mark, she and the rest of us began to sigh with relief. Unfortunately, it was only an idle reprieve and at nineteen Megan succumbed to the battle she valiantly fought for three years. Throughout it all, though the cancer had its way, Megan was very much the decision-maker, the agent, the person, and her graduation—rightfully—was the centerpiece of her own very human and very true triumph.

Another story involves me. In 1991, my dad died one month after I began teaching at Weston Jesuit School of Theology. It was a very hard time for all of us. Eight months earlier, my parents' home, along with everything that they owned, was destroyed in a fire. They rebuilt the house, sold it, and moved to Florida. They had only just picked out a condo that was being built when my dad died. After his death I was frequently flying to Florida to help my mom, I was dealing with my own grief, and I was trying to figure out how to teach at Weston.

With grief we have our good days and bad days. One day I was having a good one, until a colleague of mine stopped me in the stairwell that leads from the office building's lobby. With people passing all around me she grabbed my hand and asked me, "Jim, how are you?" I said that I was fine. "No, Jim, how are you?" "Fine, thank you," I said, now trying to get away, though she held my hand tighter. "No, Jim, how are you really?" I said, "I'm fine, thank you," and left.

I was angry and hurt. She wanted me to unleash my grief in the lobby before other colleagues, the staff, and my students. And for whose benefit? Sometimes we think the willingness to listen brings with it the right to examine or, in this case, interrogate the sufferer.

Sometimes the sufferer can communicate, in fact, loudly and clearly. They might, in fact, contradict our expectations. Here we may want to remember a claim I made in the chapter on love. There I remarked that whereas we might be called to love Christ in the neighbor, we are first called to love the neighbor as they are in themselves. Nowhere is this more remarkable than in the sufferer who faces their threats in uncannily candid ways.

The womanist theologian M. Shawn Copeland turns to the words of black slave women to see how they responded to the continuous powerful oppression of their "owners." She helps us to hear in the cry of those slave women, not necessarily words of desperation and fear, but also words of resistance, triumph, and, as Copeland puts it, sass. Through voice, sufferers articulate their own rightful resistance to suffering.

Copeland specifically turns to the voices of the black slave singing the spirituals:

> The spirituals . . . were an important resource of resistance. . . . The spirituals reshaped and conflated the characters and stories, parables and pericopes, events and miracles of the Hebrew and Christian scriptures. These songs told the mercy of God anew and testified to the ways in which the enslaved people met God at the whipping post, on the auction block, in the hush arbor, in the midnight flight to freedom. . . . If the makers of the spirituals glorified in singing of the cross of Jesus, it was not because they were masochistic and enjoyed suffering. Rather, the enslaved Africans sang because they saw in the rugged wooden planks One who had endured what was their daily portion. The cross was treasured because it enthroned the One who went all the way with them and for them. The enslaved Africans sang because they saw the result of the cross—triumph over the principalities and powers of death, triumph over evil in this world.[7]

In the spirituals we hear voices uttering a language of redemption. But Copeland introduces another way in which black women during slavery voiced their suffering through the language of resistance: "In these narratives, women model audacious behavior: wit, cunning, verbal warfare, and moral courage. These Black women *sass!* *The Random House Dictionary of the English Language* defines *sass* as 'impudent or disrespectful back talk.' Enslaved black women used sass to guard, regain, and secure self-esteem; to obtain and hold psychological distance; to speak truth; to challenge the atmosphere of moral ambiguity that surrounds them; and sometimes to protect against sexual assault."[8]

Copeland teaches us that if we want really to understand suffering we might want to listen to the experienced, articulate voice of the sufferer. Sometimes we might not hear what we might like. Perhaps we find the spirituals more acceptable than the sass. But if we silence the sass then we are not unlike those whom Scarry writes about who try to inhibit the voices of the suffering.

When the sufferer is resistant we hear another language spoken. Copeland elaborates: "A theology of suffering in a womanist perspective is resistant. With motherwit, courage, sometimes their fists and most often sass, Black women resisted the degradation of chattel slavery. . . . With sass, Black women defined themselves and dismantled the images that had been used to control and demean them. With sass, Black women turned back the shame that others tried to put on them. With sass, Black women survived, even triumphed over emotional and psychic assault."[9]

These models remind us again who are the principal agents in suffering: not ourselves nor God, but the sufferers—those who occasionally, in order to lay claim to their own universe, may at times moan, cry, sing, scream, remain silent, or even give us sass. But inevitably, by trying to voice their own concerns, they invite us into the task of seeing the threat to their universe.

Before we turn to the "meaning" of suffering, I offer three narratives about speaking through one's suffering. The first again regards my niece Megan, who suffered a rare strain of leukemia before her death at nineteen. Megan asserted herself quite clearly, especially whenever a physician, seeing her as a child, albeit at sixteen, seventeen, or eighteen years of age with a life-threatening illness, treated her as a child to be seen but not heard. Once a physician had wrongly inserted her port and he was trying to correct it by pressing powerfully against her chest. Megan moaned, cried, and asked him to stop. He ignored her and persisted more aggressively. Finally, she let loose with a set of expletives that stunned us all; my sister, brother-in-law, and I were amazed, though the nurses were elated. This doctor who showed no compassion to children was finally frightened by a child he tried to intimidate. Unfortunately for Megan, she had to stoop to his depths, but she gave him a lesson that many before her wanted to give him.

The second concerns Connie, a lawyer friend of mine and a devoted mother of three, whose middle daughter, Maureen, was an eleven-year-old fighting leukemia at the same time as Megan. She told me the story of a little eight-year-old in the hospital bed next to her daughter who was also suffering from leukemia. A nurse came in to give the girl an injection and the girl cried, "I'm afraid." "No, you're not afraid; you are a big girl," contradicted the nurse, giving the girl her injection. After the nurse left, my friend Connie went over to the girl's mother and said, "Excuse me, but I would never let a nurse or doctor contradict my child. Things are bad enough that she should have to conform her suffering to the nurse's efficiency."

On another occasion Maureen, suffering from punctured lungs, had been living for several weeks with tubes in her chest. An older woman in her room had a similar catheter. The older woman said to Maureen, "Honey, when they put that thing in your chest did they say that you would experience 'discomfort'?" "Yes," Maureen responded. "You know, discomfort is sitting in a wooden chair for twenty minutes or wearing tight shoes. That thing hanging out of your chest isn't discomfort; it's living hell." Little Maureen facing leukemia found in that woman someone who knew her suffering. But those who translated her suffering as "discomfort" were unable to listen, let alone understand the little girl's living hell.

WHAT IS SUFFERING?

Eric Cassell, author of *The Nature of Suffering*, distinguishes pain from suffering by making the simple observation that pain can exist without suffering and suffering can exist without pain. He describes suffering as "the distress brought about by the actual or perceived impending threat to the integrity or continued existence of the whole person." That is, suffering emerges when people become aware of the fact that something necessary for them is not only beyond their grasp, but also might never again be attainable. Cassell notes, therefore, that suffering arises with "the loss of the ability to pursue purpose."[10] People suffer when they actually lose some good or when they recognize they may never obtain some good that is seriously important for them to have: health, mobility, a loving marriage, a trusted friend, a decent job.

In the actual loss of a good, they recognize that their own well-being and their own general relatedness with others are also diminished. In the case of foreseeing the necessary good as unattainable, they similarly recognize their future well-being and general relatedness as also threatened. Thus, when people suffer, they find themselves marginalized from those who enjoy the very goods they have lost or were hoping would be theirs. They experience a sense of isolation, a sense that they do not have what brings others together. Not only do they feel marginalized by the loss of what was had or what was expected, but the feeling itself occurs individually and privately. Cassell writes, "Suffering is necessarily private because it is ultimately individual."[11]

Human beings are, however, enormously resourceful. When they find themselves isolated and at a loss, they develop "a drive to survive." Within that drive, they develop strategies that they pursue as goals that are alternatives to the goods and the type of relatedness that will not be theirs. Moreover, the sufferer pursues a survival strategy in which their present relationships are adapted according to whether the others—family, friends, neighbors—support them in the survival strategies.

We need therefore to appreciate that when people suffer they have four defining experiences: first, they find that they are without something necessary for their incorporation with the rest of humanity; second, their personal feeling, experience, or sense of loss heightens their perceived isolation from others; third, they search for a way to renegotiate the future of their lives so that they can recoup whatever humanity was lost in the first place; and fourth, they look to their many relationships to see who will support them on their search. On this final note, we can think of the many support groups that arise for all sorts of people who have experienced loss. People who suffer often turn to these groups to help them deal with these four experiences that accompany suffering.

RELIGIOUS RESPONSES TO SUFFERING

In his famous book *Christ*, the great Dominican theologian Edward Schillebeeckx describes how different cultures address the question of suffering. Regarding religious societies, he remarks that while each religion has a different specific response to one who suffers, they share "the fact that they give the last word to the *good*, and not to evil and suffering . . . their deepest concern is to overcome suffering."[12]

Commenting on the Jews, Schillebeeckx remarks that, in the Bible, "Israel has no problems with suffering which men bring upon themselves through their own sinfulness." But Israel "protests and guards itself against unmerited suffering." Apart from sinfulness, Israel "did not simply want to accept suffering as a *given*."[13]

We need to appreciate that, regarding sin and suffering, Israel did not believe that suffering was a punishment from God for sin. Rather, Israel believed that suffering is the natural consequence of sin: if by sin one departs from the providential way of the Lord God, one will in all likelihood get lost, run into trouble, and eventually experience hardships. The notion that God punishes the sinner is a deeply questionable Christian invention. In fact, it would seem to me that this Jewish insight of suffering as at times a natural consequence of sin is a far better way of explaining why we often experience suffering in light of sin. Attributing suffering to a "punishing" God is quite absurd, no?

Still, Israel recognizes that some suffering occurs that is not as a result of sin. In fact, Israel experiences such suffering. Schillebeeckx remarks that because of belief in God, "Israel did not hesitate to direct hard questions to God. 'Is God asleep?' asks Ps. 44:23, 26."[14] Therefore, until God delivers Israel from suffering, Israel protests over God's delay.

Christians also see God and suffering as "diametrically opposed; where God appears, evil and suffering have to yield. So there is no place for suffering." Moreover, Schillebeeckx remarks that, unlike Job's friends, Jesus "breaks with the idea that suffering necessarily has something to do with sinfulness." Looking at the description of the man born blind in John's Gospel (John 9:2f.) and the account of the murdered Galileans in Luke's Gospel (Luke 13:1–5), we see "that it is possible to draw conclusions from sin to suffering, but not from suffering to sin." That is, we cannot assume that one's suffering is due to one's sinfulness.

Schillebeeckx then turns to the Christian notion of redemptive suffering and again dismisses the notion of a Christian God who sends suffering our way. Schillebeeckx provides strong testimony regarding Christian faith and suffering that in some circles is often misunderstood. Though he acknowledges that some suffering may actually help some individuals to become more sensitive and compassionate and, in some instances, actually transform a person, still he says decisively, "there is an excess of suffering and evil in our history."

I find Schillebeeckx here very helpful. I can see someone in their own suffering trying to see its meaning in their lives, and they may at some point say that the suffering has helped them, that it is redemptive. But I find it difficult to ascribe it to another's suffering. For instance, like others, I have met parents suffering over the death of a child, migrant workers unable to care adequately for their children, the people at Smokey Mountain in the Philippines where tens of thousands literally live in a garbage dump. I have sat with people in terrible suffering from cancer or HIV/AIDS. I have read about survivors of families swept away by mudslides from typhoons, taken away in tornadoes in the Midwest or by hurricanes in the South. I have heard about earthquakes in already devastated parts of the world, floods and famine affecting people barely able to survive, refugees adrift at sea. I can think of the victims of war in Rwanda, Nigeria, Poland, Germany, the Philippines. I cannot understand why they have that suffering. I cannot call this suffering redemptive. Rather, I am struck silent.

Schillebeeckx confirms our experiences as he continues: "There is a barbarous excess, for all the explanations and interpretations. There is too much *unmerited* and *senseless* suffering for us to be able to give an ethical, hermeneutical and ontological analysis of our disaster." He surmises, "human reason cannot in fact cope with concentrated historical suffering and evil."[15] But he adds that not only human reason, but the scriptures too cannot explain away suffering. He writes:

> The Christian message does not give an *explanation* of evil or our history of suffering. That must be made clear from the start. Even for Christians, suffering remains impenetrable and incomprehensible, and provokes rebellion. Nor will the Christian blasphemously claim that God himself required the death of Jesus as compensation for what *we* make of our history.[16]

Schillebeeckx offers us, however, another way of looking at redemptive suffering and that is by giving it an ultimately liberating significance. This is the suffering that persons assume in their responsible concern to overcome others' greater suffering. Here is love electing suffering to help another, and the primary model for this love is God.

On this point, the wonderful late Presbyterian theologian William Placher describes eloquently the suffering of God:

> God suffers because God is vulnerable, and God is vulnerable because God loves—and it is love, not suffering or even vulnerability, that is finally the point. . . . The freedom of love is good, and that freedom risks suffering and, in a sinful world full of violence and injustice, will always encounter it sooner or later. Love does not regret the price it pays for making itself vulnerable, but to speak of paying a price is itself to acknowledge that the suffering is itself an evil. Vulnerability, on the other hand, is a perfection of loving freedom.[17]

We imitate God when we practice this vulnerability and its accompanying mercy, that is, the willingness to enter into the chaos of another. That merciful act often entails an elective suffering for the sake of others.

Here another Dominican, Sister Mary Catherine Hilkert, discusses the importance of solidarity with those who suffer by reflecting on the lives of the four American church women (Maura Clarke, Ita Ford, Dorothy Kazel, and Jean Donovan) who were killed in December 1980 in El Salvador. There we see the nature of one's commitment to stand in solidarity with those who suffer. We can find in these four women's testimonies how, when, and why embracing the suffering of another is an imitation of Christ, an act of vulnerable love. Hilkert writes, "These women embraced solidarity with the poor not out of any glorification or romanticization of suffering, but because it was among the poor of the world that they discovered the good news of the reign of God at work in the world despite all evidence to the contrary."[18]

Hilkert invites us to listen to these women's decisions to stand in solidarity with those who suffer. Ita Ford wrote of her decision to enter in Christ's own paschal mystery, the mystery of suffering, death, and resurrection: "Am I willing to suffer with the people here, the suffering of the powerless? Can I say to my neighbors, 'I have no solution to this situation; I don't know the answers, but I will walk with you, search with you, be with you?'"[19]

Two weeks before her death, Jean Donovan asked about how her own self was being stretched by the decision to stay in solidarity with those whom she served: "Several times I have decided to leave El Salvador. I almost could except for the children, the poor, the bruised victims of this insanity. Who would care for them? Whose heart could be as staunch as to favor the reasonable thing in a sea of their tears and loneliness? Not mine, dear friend, not mine."[20] The decision of these brave women who were brutally murdered on December 2, 1980, stands as a clear example of vulnerable love or redemptive suffering.

Reading Schillebeeckx on suffering is very helpful. He notes what all religions have in common: the religious response to suffering is to find a way of eliminating suffering. Moreover, he corrects those false impressions of Christianity (which too often Christians promote) that seem to make suffering an expression of a loving God's will, and he offers us a palpable notion of redemptive suffering but in the key of solidarity, mercy, and liberation.

But I think he leaves us short on one particular point: he trusts too much in the distinction between "merited" and "unmerited" suffering. Schillebeeckx acknowledges that the book of Job, like the Gospels of Luke and John, debunks any attempt to suggest that where there is suffering there must have been sin. Nonetheless, Schillebeeckx leaves unacknowledged the problem of the distinction between "merited" and "unmerited" suffering.

To the extent that we maintain this distinction, we believe that we can discern whose suffering is merited and whose is not. To the extent that we leave the distinction intact, we still believe that we can determine who should be beneficiaries of our compassion and who should not. But how can we know that someone's suffering is really "unmerited"? How do we arrive at such divine judgment? Does the AIDS victim have to be a child or a hemophiliac? Does the cancer victim really have to have been taking every precaution against carcinogens? Does the tortured political activist really have to have been politically prudent? Does the date-rape victim really have to be insisting "No" the entire evening?

The distinction between merited and unmerited suffering strikes me as still engaging the albeit-modified stance of the so-called friends of Job—Eliphaz, Bildad, and Zophar—who contended with Job about his "merited suffering." My point is, if we believers only stand in protest against unmerited suffering, how are we to know what is and what is not merited? And, if we insist on the distinction, it seems to me that a deep residue of moralism is apparent wherever listeners are encouraged to sift out the "merited" from "unmerited" sufferers.

For instance, have you not attended a wake and heard people whisper right by the casket: "He should have quit smoking earlier." "She should have left him years ago." "He should have had gone on that diet." "She never took care of herself." Why do we make these utterances? For whose benefit do we make them? The poor person is already dead! We are standing right there over the casket, purportedly "paying our respects" and somehow we righteously decide that we need to blame the deceased for their death. Why is it that whenever anyone dies, it is invariably their fault? "I told him he shouldn't drive that car." "If she stayed home more often, she wouldn't have been on that plane." "He should never have walked home that way." "I always have thought that microwave ovens are dangerous!"

Let us not deny that evidently some suffering is tragically unmerited, but I am sure that in many instances we have a propensity to judge another's suffering as merited. Is not the ultimate purpose of this dubious distinction to winnow out those people whom we believe are not worthy of our compassion? And are we not far harsher in our judgment than our all-seeing God is? So are we not finally left with the distinction as little more than a device that allows us to withdraw compassion and to confirm our self-serving righteousness? The distinction allows us, I think, the opportunity to parse out our sympathy in very condescending and stingy ways.

Study Questions

How do you define suffering?

From what experiences of yours, with family and friends, did you come to understand suffering better?

If God is all-loving, why do people suffer?

Do you think that a person's ability to express their suffering is necessary for healing?

PART II

THE TEXTS

Chapter Five

Jesus in the New Testament

Before we examine Jesus and God's word, let us reflect on how we think about God. I would like to try an exercise with you. Think for a moment, what is your image of God? When you pray, when you dwell on God, who is God? Have you a picture, an idea, an image?

I asked that question in 1985 of a very active international community of religious women living and working in Rome. In the community there were about twelve sisters.

As the occasional chaplain for the sisters, I was invited one time to lead a day of recollection, and I began the day asking them to share what their image of God was. I volunteered that my image was the father of the prodigal son. The principal of the school said that she always prayed to Jesus the Teacher. Another, a very charismatic woman, talked about her relationship with the Spirit. One who worked with the infirm saw God as healer, whereas another, probably the freest of us all, saw God as God.

These images are terrific—they help us approach God in prayer and in hope. The image welcomes us and, in many instances, our particular image of God helps us get closer to God. Moreover, as we get older the images of God that most affect us are those that resonate with our particular vocation. Not surprisingly, teachers see Jesus as teacher, and physicians see Jesus as healer.

But these images are also very limiting. I would go to prayer and the Father of the prodigal son could not be nicer. He was always glad to see me! I could go to prayer completely undisturbed. But the God who judges, the God who commands, and the God who is sovereign were nowhere near my image of God. I only saw a nice, rich, fatherly God who hugged me and welcomed me. Like those images of the smiling, good-looking Jesus, how could anyone fail to want to hang out with the father of the prodigal son? Why wouldn't we love just going to sit in prayer with him who will do everything for us?

In order to think rightly about God, then, we need to do three basic things. First, following the first commandment, we must recognize God's sovereignty. This means that as much as we would like to know God, God is also so great that we cannot simply reduce God to an image. Remember Moses and the burning bush? When Moses asked God what God's name was, God resisted Moses's question and answered, "I am who am." God is not going to let us simply make him into a cool idol. The sovereignty of God lets God be God.

We have to understand that the Creator, Redeemer, and Sanctifier is Someone completely beyond us. God eludes us.

Yet still we need to at least know a little about God. In order to do this, we need to try understanding God first by trying to understand what God couldn't be, as Thomas Aquinas and other Scholastics claimed. They used the *via negativa*. It is easier to know what God couldn't be, rather than what God is. God couldn't be limited, or mean, or powerless. The *via negativa* helps us to see what God is not.

Second, we also need to recognize that, because God is love, we are called into an intimate relationship with God, and to do that, we need images that allow us to receive through a mediating way the love of our sovereign God. We need then to constantly allow God's personal but sovereign (or sovereign but personal) love to enter into our lives through mediating images. In order to pray to God, we need the image of God as teacher, father of the prodigal son, as spirit, and so on, but we need to make sure that our image of God is not simply one image. We need to allow other images into our prayer; otherwise we confine our understanding of God to a minimalist understanding

Third, as we get older, we should look for images that are competitive with one another. The meek and welcoming Jesus who says "Let the children come to me" is different from the angry, principled righteous person who turns over the tables of the money-changers in the Temple. We should literally look to broaden our understanding of God.

In light of the needed tension to let God be God but to let God enter into our lives through images, let us see how the Gospels instruct us.

The Jesus of History

In theology we tend to distinguish into two categories but not to separate our understanding of Jesus: his life up to and including his death, and his life in glory after his resurrection. The categories are Jesus of history and the Christ of faith; these are two ways that we know Jesus Christ. The Jesus of history is the Jesus of the Gospels. The Christ of faith is the Lord in glory. We will look first at the Jesus of history.

One theologian writes that the scriptures exist to help us get the identity of Jesus right. This is not just a cognitional exercise or, as others would say, a head trip. Rather, we can only get the identity of Jesus right if we surrender all our safe presuppositions about Jesus and if we let Jesus just be Jesus.[1]

One person who struggled with understanding Jesus was Peter. Jesus asks Peter, "Who do people say that I am?" Peter answers, giving a host of identities, a prophet or John the Baptist. Then Jesus says, "But Peter, who do you say that I am?" Peter says, "You are the Christ, the Son of the living God." Bingo! Peter gets the title of Jesus right. But then Jesus goes on to clarify what the Son of God must do: be rejected, suffer, die, and be buried. Peter does not like this interpretation and basically tells Jesus he's wrong. Jesus responds even more forcefully, saying to Peter, "Get behind me, Satan." Peter could not get the identity of Jesus right. Peter knew that Jesus was the Christ. He just did not want the Christ to suffer and die. Peter resisted the identity of Jesus. Jesus was Jesus when he taught, cured the sick, got huge crowds, and performed miracles. Jesus was going to be a success story, or so Peter thought. Peter could not anticipate the Last Supper, the agony in the garden, the trial, and the cross. Peter is going to spend the entire Gospel narrative learning what it means for Jesus to be the Christ. Not until the resurrection did Peter begin to fathom who Jesus is. And then the evangelist John on the beach describes Jesus confronting Peter and us with what exactly it means to get the story of Jesus right. Getting the story of Jesus right means giving up, as Peter finally did, on all the safe and protective assumptions that keep us from knowing Jesus as he is.

The stories of the scriptures can transform us so that we can get the identity of Jesus right. For that to happen, we need to let the scriptures speak to us so that we can understand who Jesus is. If we let Jesus be who he is, then the scriptures will not only give us ideas, but they will actually transform us.

One of the leading liberation theologians, Father Jon Sobrino, stayed with me about one year ago. He lives in El Salvador. On November 16, 1989, in El Salvador, all the members of his community—six Jesuits and their housekeeper and her daughter—were brutally murdered. Jon was in Asia speaking when the assassinations occurred.

Jon lectured here at Boston College and his central message was that we remember the Jesus of history. Why? Because Jesus died on the cross. The one whom we call our Lord and Savior was completely abandoned and vilified. Before he became the Christ in glory, Jesus was the one hanging on a cross.

How could this happen? Why did it happen? These are questions that Sobrino asks us. These are some of the most important questions in Christian faith. How could the Lord of history end up abandoned and executed in an ignominious way?

Like others, Sobrino wants us to get the story of Jesus right. Here he takes us further. He wants us to get the story right so that we may know how to follow him—that is, to be disciples of Jesus.

We might think that the call to be a disciple of Jesus Christ is such a familiar expression that it was always a part of Christian theology, but the term applied to all Christians comes from a German theologian in the 1930s. He wrote that all Christians should understand that they are called to be disciples of Jesus.

If we get the story of Jesus right, and if we want to follow in his footsteps, what else do we need to do?

A number of theologians suggest that we need to develop the virtues in us so that we have the right stuff to follow Jesus. Understanding Jesus and following him does not just happen. We need to be able to do it! We will discuss later the need for grace and its effects, which come to us from the Christ of faith. Now we can say that there are virtues that we need to follow Jesus, to be his disciples.

Virtues promote the cultivation of interior dispositions and related practices in ourselves. To determine which virtues we should develop, contemporary virtue ethicists often offer three key questions for consideration: Who are we? Who are we called to become? How do we get there? These three questions are about our self-understanding, our goal, and the way to the goal.

Because the scriptures are really about the life, testimony, and vision of Jesus, we turn to the second question of who we ought to become. Starting at this point is appropriate; after all, we believe that we are made in Jesus's image and that we are called to become more like him.

What are the virtues that Jesus has? First, he is loving. He teaches us to love God, ourselves, and one another. Second, he is obedient to the Father's will. Third, he is merciful.

Answering the question of who we ought to become (that is, imitators of Jesus) leads us back to the first virtue question: Who are we? If we are called to follow Jesus, are we loving, do we seek to know God's will, are we merciful? These questions that pertain to our self-understanding are key. If we want to follow Jesus we need to see whether we have the virtues that he had.

The third question asks, how do we get from where we are to where Jesus is? And that's the task of the rest of this book! Still, let's start with one virtue that we need to develop.

When we ask what virtue we most need to imitate Jesus, I believe the answer to this is mercy. Mercy is Christianity's trademark: by mercy God saved us; by mercy we follow in Jesus's footsteps.

The claim that mercy is the Christian's trademark merits attention. As we will see in chapter 7, several sources validate the claim, but at this point one text in particular summons us. Still, to get to that text, I need first to say a word about my colleague, friend, and coauthor Dan Harrington, who reads and writes more than anyone I know in theology.[2] To date, besides the thirty-odd books that he has written or edited, he has authored thirty thousand reviews for the journal he edits, *New Testament Abstracts*.

Being so well-read, he is the ideal colleague. I ask, "Dan, should I read this book?" "No, just catch the preface; it explains everything." "Dan, should I read this new work on Paul and ethics?" "No, pages 220 through 227 are very important and sufficient." "Dan, what about this new article on Luke and women?" "The last two paragraphs are very well done." Imagine my surprise when he said, "Jim, you should read Rodney Stark's *The Rise of Christianity*." "Which parts?" I asked, having now been well-trained. "The whole thing."

In *The Rise of Christianity*, Stark argues that "Christianity was an urban movement, and the New Testament was set down by urbanites."[3] Those urban areas were dreadful. Stark describes the conditions in those areas as "social chaos and chronic urban misery." This chaos resulted in part from population density. At the end of the first century, Antioch's population was 150,000 within the city walls, or 117 persons per acre. By way of comparison, New York City has a density of thirty-seven persons per acre, and Manhattan with its high-rise apartments has one hundred persons per acre. Moreover, contrary to common assumptions, Greco-Roman cities were not settled places whose inhabitants descended from previous generations. With high infant mortality and relatively brief life expectancy, these cities required "a constant and substantial stream of newcomers" in order to maintain their population levels. As a result, the cities were largely comprised of strangers. These strangers were well-treated by early Christians, many of whom, again contrary to assumptions, were anything but poor. Through a variety of ways of caring for newcomers, financially secure Christians welcomed the newly arrived immigrants.

Moreover, their religion was new. Certain demands were imposed by the gods of the pagan religions. But these demands were substantively ritual; they were not neighbor-directed. And while pagan Romans knew generosity, that generosity did not stem from any divine command. A nurse who cared for a victim of an epidemic knew that her life might be lost. If she were a pagan, there was no expectation of divine reward for her generosity; if she were a Christian, however, she believed that she would be rewarded in the next life for having done what God commanded in this life.

The religion was new to the Roman Empire, therefore, because the Christian God required mercy to be practiced toward all who called upon the name of the Lord. Christianity required the recognition of the stranger in need as neighbor and, inevitably, as sibling; Christianity commanded the Christian to embrace faithfully the one in need of mercy. Stark writes:

> This was the moral climate in which Christianity taught that mercy is one of the primary virtues—that a merciful God requires humans to be merciful. Moreover, the corollary (that *because* God loves humanity, Christians may not please God unless they *love one another*) was entirely new. Perhaps even more revolutionary was the principle that Christian love and charity must extend beyond the boundaries of family and tribe, that it must extend to "all those who in every place call on the name of our Lord Jesus Christ" (1 Cor. 1:2). . . . This was revolutionary

stuff. Indeed, it was the cultural basis for the revitalization of a Roman world groaning under a host of miseries.[4]

We will see more on this later, but at the end of the Good Samaritan parable, Jesus asks the scribe, "Who is neighbor?" The scribe answers, "The one who showed mercy." Jesus responds, "Go and do likewise." Heeding his command, the early Christians became, through mercy, effective witnesses to the claims of the Gospels.

THE CHRIST OF FAITH

For Christians, the life of Jesus does not end with the cross. We believe that Jesus is raised from the dead, not as in a resuscitation, but as in living eternally in glory. He is the first born of the new creation.

We believe that we too will be raised in glory, but we also believe that along the way of discipleship, the Christ of history helps us. One fundamental way that we are assisted is by faith: the Christ of faith gives us faith. Faith is a gift. We do not believe because we simply decide to believe. Rather, we receive from Christ the invitation to believe, and from Christ we receive the grace, the divine ability, to believe.

In faith then we follow Jesus Christ. Yet even the call to follow Jesus and even the ability to be a disciple come from Christ. He calls us to follow him; he gives us the grace to follow him. In short, Christ makes it possible for us to follow him.

Certainly we need to give our assent to the call of Christ to follow him, but the call itself is first from God. God wills us to follow Christ. We are called. But then in order to be good disciples we need God's assistance and this is what grace is about—the divine gift to help us on the way to salvation.

Three gifts of grace are the virtues of faith, hope, and charity. By faith we are able to believe in God and in Jesus Christ. Faith is the foundation of the Christian life: by faith we believe in the Trinity, our creation, the incarnation, redemption, the true nature of Jesus Christ, the kingdom of God, and eternal life.

Hope is to have confidence for things not yet seen. Hope, too, is a gift. Sometimes people think of Christian hope as what we have in light of success. But Christian hope is our aid in the face of adversity. By hope, we believe we will attain what even now seems so unattainable. I think it is important to see that Christian hope begins at the cross of Jesus. We are not foolish in hope; rather, we are realists. We understand the challenges of life, but we believe that by hope we can meet and overcome those challenges.

Finally, we receive charity as a gift as well. Charity is the experience of being in union with God, oneself, and one another. Jesus gave us a command to love, but charity makes it possible for us to follow that command.

The Christ of faith also is accompanied by the Holy Spirit. We remember from the scriptures that after the death and resurrection of Jesus, the Holy Spirit descended onto the disciples at Pentecost and gave them the ability to believe, to hope, and to love. The Holy Spirit accompanies us as we follow the Lord of history.

Together these virtues make us free to follow Christ and to do the will of God. We are made free by these gifts of grace. And here we return to the beginning of this chapter because it is important to realize that only after the death and resurrection of Jesus, and then the descent of the Holy Spirit, does Peter get the narrative right. No matter how hard Peter tried, it was only with the grace of Christ in glory and the assistance of the Holy Spirit that Peter would be able to understand what it meant for Jesus to be the Christ. Once Peter understood that, Peter was free to preach Jesus Christ and to follow him.

Years ago a professor of mine from the Gregorian University in Rome, Father Klaus Demmer, MSC, taught me that inevitably the scriptures must have a real, transforming effect on us, or else Christ died in vain. I think this is very important, because it asks us to answer the question: Do I understand that Jesus died for me?

When we answer that we do, we find ourselves on the way of Jesus. By getting the narrative of Jesus right, we hear the call and find our lives transformed.

STUDY QUESTIONS

What is your (main) image of God? Why do you think it is so important for you?

Do you believe that Jesus died for you? What does this mean?

Jesus calls you to be his disciple. What does discipleship mean to you?

There have been numerous movies about Jesus: The Passion of the Christ, Jesus of Nazareth, King of Kings, The Greatest Story Ever Told, Jesus of Montreal, *and so on. Which movie have you found to be a good way of treating the life, death, and resurrection of Jesus?*

What do you think of the distinction between the Jesus of history and the Christ of faith?

Chapter Six

THE TEN COMMANDMENTS
IN THE CATECHISM

In the United States, one of the greatest Christian ethicists is James Gustafson. He has influenced the field, directing doctoral candidates in Christian ethics at Yale, Chicago, and Emory universities. Gustafson proposes two perspectives on how to best understand the New Testament, by way of revealed morality and revealed reality.[1]

Reading the New Testament through the lens of revealed morality means that we are seeking to figure out if the text "reveals" a new code of ethics by which we should live. Certainly, the New Testament gives us the new law. It promulgates the love commandment (Matt. 22:34–40; Mark 12:28–34; Luke 10:25–28). But does it reveal many other ethical and moral codes? Jesus, for instance, says no divorce (Mark 10:11–12; Luke 16:18), but then Matthew's Gospel raises an exception (Matt. 5:31–32), and later Paul raises his own as well (1 Cor. 7:12–16). Is this revealed morality?

What about dietary laws? After all, the Old Testament had over six hundred laws and many of them were dietary. Are these revealed laws, laws of revealed morality? Or what about sex before marriage? Is there any revealed morality about this issue in the New Testament? Or even on abortion? A long line of questions arise, including: Should women be treated equal to men? Should children be treated in a particular way? Again and again the question arises: Where are the New Testament laws about the issues we face every day?

As we ask more and more questions about contemporary issues, like stem-cell research, cloning, gender equity, class differentiation, democratic values, and so on, we find fewer and fewer instances of the scriptures instructing us with laws of revealed morality.

With all these questions and so few clear answers, many moral theologians look at the other alternative as providing a better context for understanding how God's will is conveyed. They talk about a revealed reality in which our lives and our world are illuminated by the Gospels. Here we are invited to look at reality in a new way: the mercy of God redeeming the world through the life, death, and resurrection of Jesus. Then, in the light of God's revelation, we formulate our code of ethics through our reason, experience, and long tradition.

So which alternative do you prefer? Revealed morality with laws straight from God? Or revealed reality that provides a context for articulating the laws that we believe God wants us to live by?

Fortunately, by being Roman Catholics we do not have to choose because Catholics invariably avoid "either/or" options and pursue instead "both/and" approaches. We recognize clearly that our world is illuminated by the Gospels and that we live in a time that is already the reign of God, though not yet. But we also see that, as a matter of fact, God's will is clearly expressed in a variety of utterances: for instance, the love commandment and the works of mercy in the Last Judgment (Matt. 25:31–46). Moreover, there are some from the Old Testament that need to be recognized for the formation of the Christian moral life. Among these, the Ten Commandments has a priority of place.

It is important to examine the Ten Commandments carefully, in order to discern how they contribute to both our understanding of God and our moral wisdom. In the following section, I address three questions: How did the Ten Commandments enter into the tradition of moral wisdom? How were they used? And how can they be used today? I conclude with a postscript about law and rights.

THE TEN COMMANDMENTS AND THE
TRADITION OF MORAL THEOLOGY

We have already seen that from the fifth to the nineteenth century, the history of moral theology has been almost exclusively dominated by the concern to assist priests in the proper administration of the sacrament of penance. But moving from the "penitentials" of the early Middle Ages to the "confessional manuals" of high Scholasticism to, finally, the "moral manuals" of modern times, we find a number of developments worth noting.

For instance, when the penitentials were formulated from the fifth to the twelfth century, they were concerned about one main thing: giving penances with equity. It was believed then (though it is not the common practice today) that if you confessed to a night of debauchery, you should get the same penance as the others who were with you. Aiming to assign such equitable penances, these pamphlets were given the name "penitentials." For this reason a confessor was "good" during these centuries for his just or equitable judgments.

How were these penances organized in the penitentials? The abbots who wrote these pamphlets shaped them around the seven deadly sins. If a penitent came to a confessor, the confessor would have his penitential pamphlets in which sins were listed under the template of lust, pride, gluttony, sloth, envy, anger, avarice. Then, according to the gravity and frequency of the sinful act, a corresponding penance was assigned.

By the twelfth century, there was a change. Abelard (1079–1142), Bernard of Clairvaux (1090–1153), Hildegard of Bingen (1098–1179), and other Europeans were awakening to a sense of being a person with unique experiences, or the concept of "interiority," as we call it today. In the twelfth century, terms like *person, image of God,* and *intentionality* emerged in a whole new way. As a result, administering the sacrament of penance became much more complex. New questions arose. What if a person committed a sinful act but did not fully mean it? Or what if she was misled into sin? Or worse, what if he was forced? Questions of intentionality, ignorance, and freedom emerged at the end of the twelfth century and new texts were required.

Moreover, we recall that at the beginning of the thirteenth century, Innocent III (1160–1216) imposed the Easter duty on the church. With all Christians having to confess at least annually, priests needed more comprehensive manuals.

Finally, the self-understanding of the confessor expanded: he is not only to be a just judge giving out equitable penances; now he is also to be the physician of the soul, investigating the interior causes of the sickness of sin and prescribing correct remedies against sin's contagion.

As a result of these needs, new comprehensive confessional manuals arose in the twelfth century and dominated moral theology until the sixteenth century—they probed with medical acuity the state of the human soul. Despite their innovation, these much larger manuals still used the categories of the seven deadly sins.

Before the Reformation in the sixteenth century, a number of theologians began to question the privileged position of the seven deadly sins. One key figure is John Gerson (1363–1429), who wanted to provide a more positive, scripture-based formation to Christians and to overcome the minimalist claims of simply avoiding sin. Gerson turned to the Ten Commandments, which he called "the rock of Christian Ethics." His main context for the instruction on the Ten Commandments was a "catechism," and he and others began putting together these accessible, yet somewhat comprehensive, books of Christian instruction.

A century later, during the Reformation, Martin Luther (1483–1546) and John Calvin (1509–1564), and then the fathers of the Council of Trent (1545–1547, 1551–1552, 1562–1563) used the Ten Commandments as the basis of moral instruction in the context of catechetical instruction. Their appeal to the Ten Commandments was itself a repudiation of the primacy accorded to the seven deadly sins, and this for several reasons. First, because they were in the scriptures, the commandments and not the deadly sins claimed to be revealed morality; they enjoyed the biblical warrant of expressing God's will. Second, unlike the seven deadly sins, they offered not only negative prohibitions but, on occasion, positive prescriptions. Not only do they prohibit killing and stealing, but they impose on us the duty to honor God, God's name, the Sabbath, and our parents. Finally, with the possible exception of pride, the deadly sins were primarily offensive to human life alone. The commandments, however, specified prescriptions and prohibitions that begin with our relationship with God and moved from there to our relationships with one another.

It is helpful to see an example of how the commandments were used. Martin Luther's *Large Catechism* (1529) dedicated nearly half of its 120 pages to the Ten Commandments. Generally speaking in terms of prohibitions or prescriptions, Luther began his instruction of each commandment by following the specific form of the commandment, but then turned to its corollary. If the commandment was a prohibition, he treated the prohibition first, but then considered its prescriptive features. The fifth commandment on killing began, for instance, with an explanation of the prohibition, but turned eventually to consider the failure to do good to one's neighbor: "God rightly calls all persons murderers who do not offer counsel and aid to men in need and in peril of body and life."

Furthermore, Luther's explanations focused not on particular external actions that were in themselves right or wrong, but rather on interior dispositions and particular relationships. That is, more than focusing on particular actions that were outlawed, Luther considered the vices that gave birth to some actions.

Finally, the heart dominated Luther's interpretation of the commandments. He concludes the first commandment: "Where the heart is right with God and this commandment is kept, fulfillment of all the others will follow of its own accord."

In that same year Luther published the *Small Catechism*, which was designed so that the head of the household could handily instruct his Christian family. The three features in the *Large Catechism* remained in the *Small Catechism*: matching prohibition and prescription; emphasizing habitual, relational conduct; and acting always from a charitable heart. For instance, the eighth commandment is simply "We should fear and love God so that we do not deceitfully belie, betray, backbite, nor slander our neighbor, but apologize for him, speak well of him, and put the most charitable construction on all that he does."

The Ten Commandments became then the staple of the moral tradition in every major denominational movement of the sixteenth century. Roman Catholics as well as the followers of Martin Luther and John Calvin recognized in the Ten Commandments a moral foundation that was biblically based, had both prescriptions and prohibitions, asserted the priority of the interior disposition over the exterior action, and began with our relationship with God and moved to our relationship with one another. Indeed, the Ten Commandments were recognized again as "the rock of Christian Ethics."

Here they are as taught by the Catholic Church today:

1. I am the Lord your God, you shall not have strange gods before me.
2. You shall not take the name of the Lord your God in vain.
3. Remember to keep holy the Lord's Day.
4. Honor your father and your mother.
5. You shall not kill.
6. You shall not commit adultery.
7. You shall not steal.
8. You shall not bear false witness against your neighbor.
9. You shall not covet your neighbor's wife.
10. You shall not covet your neighbor's goods.

How Were the Ten Commandments Used?

After the Reformation, Catholics incorporated the Ten Commandments not only into their catechisms but also into their new moral manuals. Indeed, if the twelfth century marks a break with the penitentials, the sixteenth century marks a break with the confessional manuals.

After the Council of Trent, seminaries were established that required, among other innovations, the formal study of moral theology. With these courses came the need for textbooks, and as a result the moral manuals were developed from the sixteenth to the twentieth century. Of course, like their forerunners, these manuals remain singularly concerned with sin. But now the moral manuals use the Ten Commandments to analyze contemporary cases. What did these moral manuals look like?

One of the first Jesuit moral manuals was by Francisco de Toledo (1532–1596).[2] In 1569, Toledo was made preacher of the papal court and, then, theologian of the Sacred Penitentiary and the Roman Inquisition, and consultor to several Roman congregations. In time, he served seven popes. He was made cardinal in 1593, the first Jesuit to receive that honor.[3]

Toledo developed his manual from his teaching theology at the Roman College (later known as the Gregorian University) from 1562 to 1569. The manual is divided into seven books: priesthood, the administration of the sacraments, the practice of confession, the first three commandments, the remaining seven, the six precepts of the church, and matrimony. After finally being published in 1598, it went through seventy-two editions and multitudinous translations, remaining in print until 1716.[4]

Rather than going into details, we should try to get an overview of Toledo's concerns by looking at the commandments themselves. In simply counting the number of pages dedicated to the specific commandments, the seventh commandment was by far the most important. While nineteen pages were devoted to the fifth commandment on killing, and eighteen to the fourth on honoring parents, and a mere twelve to the sixth commandment on sex, eighty-eight pages were dedicated to the seventh commandment. Similarly, the eighth commandment consisted of thirty-one pages and the ninth (today's tenth) commandment, a surprising thirty-five pages. His evident disinterest with sexual matters was reiterated as he dismissed the matter of the tenth (today's ninth) commandment by simply stating that it was treated under the sixth.[5]

His treatment of the seventh to the ninth commandments concerned social conduct. Rather than being about simple personal or even private acts of theft, lying, or concupiscence, their subject matter was about the structures of relationships in civil and ecclesiastical societies. For the seventh commandment, he examined the fundamental structures of financial institutions. After an introduction, he spent eleven chapters (17–27) on restitution, that is, the social repair of an act of theft. Then he turned to usury,[6] and after four chapters (28–31) on it, he discussed mutual compensation (*lucrum in mutuo*) for loans in three chapters (32–34), restitution of gains accrued from usury in three chapters (35–37), and the innovative public pawn shops turned Franciscan commercial banks (*de monte Pietatis*) in four chapters (38–41). His longest section (42–49) was dedicated to annuities (*census*), and he concluded his comments (50–55) on the seventh commandment on credit agencies (*cambium*).

After these chapters, the eighth commandment focused on the duties in a court of law. A chapter was dedicated to each of the different functionaries in the court: the accused, the state, witnesses, advocates, notaries, and procurators. The final chapters were about what would constitute detraction.

Though he described the ninth commandment as about the social impact of avarice,[7] actually it was about the financial responsibilities of the bishops and clergy. After extensive comments (72–75) on stipends, he turned to six chapters (76–81) on benefices. He concluded the fifth book with two chapters (82–83) on pensions and ten (84–93) on simony—that is, the buying and selling of spiritual benefits.

In examining the actual contents of Toledo's manual, we find none of the traits of the later moral manuals of the nineteenth and twentieth centuries that implicitly depicted, as John Mahoney claimed in his *The Making of Moral Theology*, highly individualistic Roman Catholic penitents obsessed with the law and worried over moral lapses, especially regarding sexual activity. A crippling narcissistic anxiety ran through those pages, which spend their time parsing dubious, scrupulous, and uncertain consciences that were more worried about their private activities than the needs of their neighbor. In Toledo's manual, we find instead a robust social consciousness, a clergy interested in understanding the relevant circumstances of human activity, and a church much more concerned with ascertaining the legitimacy of social practices within existing civil and ecclesial institutions. It might be worth our consideration today.

USING THE TEN COMMANDMENTS TODAY

How should we use the commandments today? Rather than survey all ten of them, I will present three commandments, with each one being analyzed from a different context. In this way we can appreciate just how much reflection we could generate on these ten simple laws. Thus, I examine the first commandment in a specifically biblical context, the third through a historical context, and the fourth through a contemporary experiential one. My point is that just as Toledo developed a magisterial work explicating and applying the Ten Commandments, we too can provide the contemporary Christian with considerable moral wisdom by considering the text of the Ten Commandments.

In order to understand the first commandment, we should remember that the Jews never really thought of the suffering that befell them as emitting from a punishing God. Rather, they saw anything that happened to them after they sinned as an extension or as an after effect of their sin. If they found themselves rejected from the community for having borne false witness, they believed that the rejection was not a punishment from God, but rather the simple effect of their having borne false witness.

This way of looking at morality and the world is rather natural and helpful. It makes clear that the moral code for the Jewish people was something naturally good for them. The code was not some standard that God set so that God could see who was good or bad in God's eyes. For the Jews, God was never like some dog trainer who kept raising the stick and giving a biscuit to each dog that jumped high enough. Rather, the law that God gave was a law not primarily for God's benefit and delight, but for ours. Through the law, we could become freer and happier.

In the Christian tradition many theologians argued in a similar way. Thomas Aquinas, for instance, held that nothing bothered God about human conduct except when human beings brought harm on themselves: "God is offended by the action of human beings only when they act against their own welfare."[8] What offended God was not really disobedience to the law; God was not like some temperamental lawgiver who became insulted whenever God's wishes and commands were not heeded. Thomas believed that our well-being has always been the aim of the love and wisdom of God.

For some reason we have lost this insight. We have thought of the law as something "imposed" for God's own preferences. While some of us have thought of God's law as an extension of the ego of the lawmaker who likes to know that he is in command, others have thought of God as the lawmaker who is like that pesky patrol cop who is just waiting around the bend to capture anyone going over a ridiculously low speed limit. But God's law is not for God's entertainment, but rather for our benefit.

Here it might be good for us to realize though that these are commandments. They are not simply recommendations or invitations. They are, if you will, God's orders. God orders us to keep holy on the Lord's day, to honor our parents, to not bear false witness. These are not orders which depend on whether we acknowledge them as such. They exist from God, by God's authority, and for us to obey. As commands they might go contrary to our understanding of a loving God. But God loves us and therefore gives us these commandments and they are not for negotiation.

The Ten Commandments are a rock, then, because they express the providential sovereignty of God. When we read the account in Exodus of Moses's reception of the Ten Commandments, we see how clearly the question of God's sovereignty and God's providential care are one (Exod. 20:1–17; Deut. 5:1–22). There, Moses goes up the mount trembling because he is going to encounter the God of Israel. Only by recognizing the powerful care of God can the Israelites dedicate themselves trustfully to God's own guidance. And so God establishes God's own sovereignty in their midst, precisely for their benefit.

Obeying and heeding the Ten Commandments is then a way of entering into the presence of our caring and giving God. Like Moses on the mountain, through the commands themselves we get a glimpse of our providential God, but that glimpse is only to a people of faith who recognize the sovereignty of God and of God's name.

We need to reclaim the first commandment's call to the sovereignty of God. This may be difficult, though this was not always the case.

When I grew up as a child in Brooklyn, I understood Roman Catholicism primarily in terms of sacramental and devotional practices. We wanted to get into God's presence, through the mass, benediction, confession, communion, the rosary, the lives of the saints—that is, through a variety of events in which the church mediated the presence of the divine. Our existence was rooted in the sacramental presence of a God who, while above or transcendent, was still very near.

Today, to be a Catholic lacks so much of that vertical relationship with God. Instead, it focuses on our humanity and our morality.

We have become a part of the moral majority. Today we are primarily known not for our sacramental life, but for the moral absolutes that we hold: on divorce, homosexuality, abortion, euthanasia, and birth control. Fixed on maintaining the so-called continuity of our moral teachings, we have lost our bearings regarding the divine. Of course, some think that we need to humanize these teachings, and perhaps that is right. But before we do that, before we attend (yet again) to our moral teachings; we need to return to that Catholic instinct that at once revered the sovereignty of God and still testified to God's intimate proximity. Only by "rediscovering" the primacy of the first commandment will we ever recognize the near idolatry that we attach to our observance of our moral teachings. We need to restore to our practices an indebtedness to the inimitable sovereignty of God.

When we turn to the third commandment, a little history can help.[9] In the Old Testament, the commandment appears primarily as a command to imitate God, who rested on the Sabbath. Interestingly, the early Christians did *not* rest on Saturday—the Sabbath—because they were distinguishing themselves from the Jewish people. But they also did not rest on Sunday. On the contrary, lest they be understood as idle members of the Roman Empire, they worked as everyone else did on Sunday.

Still, in the first centuries, the Church Fathers encouraged participation in the Eucharist and the divine office without invoking the third commandment. In fact, the commandment and Sunday worship were not originally considered a perfect match. Sabbath observance was a command to imitate God, the Creator who rested on the Sabbath; Sunday observance was a celebration of Jesus's death, Resurrection, and glory.

While the early church resisted Sabbath observance, the emperor Constantine imposed Sunday observance by calling for a cessation of all forms of work, except farming. Then, in the sixth century, the Council of Orleans (538) and later Martin of Braga (d. 580) articulated a prohibition against "servile work." This law was not an imposition or a burden on the serfs themselves; they welcomed the rest and the call to celebrate and to participate in the Christian community. This law was, instead, an imposition on those who owned and controlled the serfs: they now had to let their serfs rest, celebrate the Lord's day, and be gathered into the same faith community of which they were members. The move was extraordinary, for the most marginalized were now incorporated into the community and were also educated by the scriptures. They now belonged to a community in which they previously had not been free enough to participate. The "obligation" then was a liberating one: Sunday observance signified their freedom. Tangibly, Sunday was a foretaste of the promised freedom of the Lord, who has already freed all of us from sin and death.

Centuries later we would forget all this, particularly why "servile work" was originally prohibited. Instead, we developed all sorts of arguments for distinguishing servile work from other forms of permitted work. Servile work no longer meant the work of the serf; it simply meant menial work that should not be done.

The third commandment, as it was originally applied in the church, was a call to be hospitable. In summoning us to observe the Lord's day, it challenges us to participate in the very nature of God as the Creator who rests, the Redeemer who celebrates, and the Sanctifier who gathers. In that triune action we are no longer passive recipients of God's grace, but rather active participants in the Lord's nature, *keeping* the Lord's day holy for all who call upon the name of the Lord.

As the church once had the vision to assure the serfs a place in the church, we have no less a charge today to make the church a place where others encounter a welcome and a dignity not found elsewhere. What would our church look like if it were to welcome *all* people to its table? How would it look were we to actively and regularly welcome people who are poor or emotionally and mentally fragile; women who have had abortions; gays and lesbians who are in loving, committed relations; divorced but remarried persons struggling for their second or third time in marriage? I am not speaking here about changing church teaching; I'm referring instead to how we can and, I think, should welcome all people, especially to worship

Or what about our attention to those of other races? A colleague of mine, Father Bryan Massingale, recently tried to find out what Roman Catholic moral theologians had to say about racism during the civil rights movement in the 1960s and 1970s. Massingale found only one reference.[10] Though it is hard to imagine what could be worse than the fact that there was no discussion during the first twenty years of the civil rights movement by Catholic moralists, still the one reference bears examination. It was in answer to the question of whether an African American, who tried to attend mass at his own parish church but found himself barred from entering it because of his race, was still obliged to find a church elsewhere to fulfill his obligation. The moral theologians, both Jesuits, never commented on the racist parish. That entry was the only acknowledgment of racial struggles, a clear indication of how much we have forgotten the original application of the third commandment.

Ask almost anyone what the fourth commandment means and they will say: "Obey your parents." Peculiar, no? The commandment says "honor your parents," but we translate it as "obey your parents."

We think the fourth commandment calls us to obey because we learned it that way. The first virtue we were taught was the virtue of obedience. It is the virtue that parents, teachers, and babysitters dream and hope every child acquires. Obedience makes a child easier to teach and so the lesson of obedience precedes all others.

By the time we get to the lesson of the Ten Commandments, we have already learned the fourth, but we learn it as "obey." I am not complaining that early in life we learn a corruption of the fourth commandment. That obedience lesson is an important one and because of it we learn many others. Today, however, especially because we live longer, we should return to the original language of honor.

Until recently, we did not think it ordinary for a family to survive three generations. Now we are moving toward the expectation of at least four generations, if not five. Whereas before children did not even meet their grandparents, now they know their great-grandparents. Now sons and daughters know their parents not only for twenty or thirty years, but fifty or sixty years. Whereas before people knew their parents up until the beginning of their own adult-hood and were obedient to them, now we know our parents for de-cades longer and need to honor them.

Honor is a very adult virtue. I learned about honor from my dad. I have to remind you that neither parent was terribly keen on me (the firstborn) leaving home at seventeen to enter the Jesuits. But eventually we all got used to it.

When I was ordained twelve years later, I worked for two suc-cessive summers at St. Francis Xavier Church in downtown Man-hattan. Every Sunday my dad would make an hour-long drive from Long Island to hear me preach. Later, when I taught at Fordham, he journeyed to the university church whenever I preached, and when I took a parish call on Long Island, he came there, too. He did not come to give me extra support or to teach me anything. He came to listen to me, to honor me. It was then that I learned to honor some-one by listening to them.

My dad and I had a wonderful relationship, but it was not until his last years that I learned to honor him. A year before he died at the age of sixty-two, he had open-heart surgery. It was at that time I considered his mortality and it was frightening. I told my spiritual director, who in turn gave me great advice: "Talk with your dad, listen to his stories, learn more about him; you don't know how long you have him."

I learned new stories not only about his work, but also about him. On occasion I would ask him what his family was like. I knew his mom, but his dad died before I was born. He would tell me sto-ries of his mom's anxieties and the difficulties they caused him and his sister. He would tell me how poor he and my mom were in their early years of marriage and how they looked for a variety of jobs to supplement his income.

After my dad died, my mom began telling me her stories. She talks about the way she changed high schools, the jobs she had and the better ones she found, and her ambitions and desires to move about. She tells me how she loved working at St. Francis College, how she and my dad met, how they dated, and how he took piano lessons (this stunned me). She talks about death: her dad's during her childhood, her son's (my brother's), her husband's (my dad's), and now her granddaughter's (my niece's).

Her stories were filled with details, more than my dad ever provided. They were above all touching, wonderfully ordinary narratives that told me more about her than any impressions I ever had. These stories had been alive in her memory and now are in my own as well.

I know now how little I really knew my folks. I realize now that all the categories that I created to understand my parents were nothing more than the deep and lasting impressions of a child. I thought I knew them, but I only knew them through the filtered experiences of a child's mind. Even in my adult years I kept seeing their actions as extensions of those same old categories in which I so astutely placed my parents. Now I realize that the only way I can know who they are is by listening to them, by no longer presuming that I really know them so well, and by willingly asking them to tell me about themselves.

The fourth commandment is not only for my parents' sake. It is for my own as well. When we understand that we are called to honor our parents, no matter how old they are or how old we are, we understand once again how much sustained reflection on the commandments brings us in touch with God's will, which is clearly for our benefit. Heeding the commandments leads us not to a burdened life but to our destiny of well-being in love.

A Postscript on Law and Rights

The language of the commandments reminds us of the language of law, and today many of our laws are about rights. In many circles we hear Catholic scholars say things like "rights language is not church language." Or "the language of rights belongs to the Enlightenment, but not to the church." The historian Brian Tierney offers us a timely corrective that makes such utterances no longer credible.

In *The Idea of Natural Rights: Studies on Natural Rights, Natural Law, and Church Law 1150–1625*, Tierney argues that long before such momentous events as the signing of the Magna Carta, the instinct of the church was to articulate and defend the rights of individual persons.[11] While the Stoics and Cicero had earlier claimed that natural law was found in its universal, objective expressions, twelfth-century church canonists developed that insight considerably and defined the natural law as a personal force, faculty, or power inherent in individual human persons. Concerned to protect individuals, these early canonists developed the first expressions of natural rights from an understanding of the person as rational, self-aware, and morally responsible. In fact, contrary to the claims of many, Tierney claims that "medieval society was saturated with a concern for rights."[12]

Later, John Gerson proposed a reform of the church as a whole that depended on the respect of its individual members. Like William Ockham (1288–1347) and the canonists before him, Gerson presumed a correspondence and not a contradiction between personal natural rights and the common good.

Tierney investigates later writers and finds significant maturity of the idea in the writings of the Spanish Dominicans, particularly Francisco de Vitoria (1480–1546) and Bartolomé de Las Casas (d. 1566), who, while reflecting on the Spanish conquest of the New World, insisted that natural rights inhered in human persons. Las Casas, in particular, used these insights to defend the rights of American natives against their European conquerors.

In providing an account for the roots of natural rights, Tierney brilliantly confirms the suspicions of those who have thought that our contemporary society needs not a repudiation of the idea of human rights, but rather an appreciation of the deeply rational, responsible, and communal origins of personal natural rights. But he also demonstrates how the church saw that the only way to attain justice and the common good was to recognize and articulate the rights of its members. That insight into justice is precisely the same insight that Moses grasped as he received the Ten Commandments.

Study Questions

How did you learn the Ten Commandments?

Do you think that we should worship God on Sunday, or do you think it's up to the person to decide one way or another? In other words, do you believe that there is a commandment to honor God on the Lord's day? Or is it simply a personal choice?

Which commandment do you find to be the most important?

Which commandment(s) are the hardest to follow?

Do you think that other people in your generation know the Ten Commandments? If they do know them, could they name them?

Chapter Seven

PRACTICING THE
CORPORAL WORKS OF MERCY

Is there something about Catholic morality that distinguishes it from the morality of other religious believers? This is a vexing question. This is not a question about superiority. It is simply a question about distinctiveness or uniqueness. In a word, it is the question about *identity*, about what identifies us as Catholics in our moral living.

The question is vexing because it is difficult to find one thing that belongs to Catholics as Catholics. For instance, we Catholics appreciate the natural law. But, in Romans 1, Saint Paul says that the natural law is written in everyone's heart; by that law, people can tell right from wrong. Because of this, many Catholics believe that what is right for Catholics is right for everyone and whatever is wrong for Catholics is equally wrong for everyone.

Others root our morality in the scriptures. Here we think, of course, of the Ten Commandments. But these are shared with Jews, Protestants, and the Orthodox Christians. Moreover, these commandments are pretty comprehensive. From them we receive moral guidance regarding the sovereignty of God and God's name; worship; honoring parents; cherishing life, our bodies, and the truth; respecting neighbors, their families, and their property. The commandments cover most moral topics.

Despite the fact that the natural law provides all human beings access to the same moral standards and that the Ten Commandments offer those of us in the Judeo-Christian tradition a fundamental morality that has affected the foundations of morality throughout the Western world, still I want to say unequivocally that we Catholics have defined ourselves distinctively in our moral lives and that distinctiveness is found in the virtue of mercy. While in the most recent generations we may not have formed ourselves as explicitly according to mercy (which I define as the willingness to enter into the chaos of others so as to answer them in their need), still, as we shall see, the life of the Catholic Church has been to form us according to mercy.

While fellow Protestants recognize the extraordinary importance of mercy as the basic stance of our God toward us, we Catholics have taken that insight further in terms of a long legacy of the corporal works of mercy—feed the hungry, give drink to the thirsty, shelter the homeless, clothe the naked, visit the sick, visit the imprisoned, and bury the dead—and the spiritual works of mercy—give good counsel, teach the ignorant, admonish sinners, console the afflicted, pardon offenses and injuries, bear offenses patiently, and pray for the living and the dead. Those works have distinguished us, for if there is one dimension of the Christian tradition that differentiates Protestants from Catholics, it is precisely "works."

Mercy in the Catholic Tradition

To make my case for the central distinctiveness of mercy, I want to give four instances that highlight the centrality of mercy.

First, the Good Samaritan parable portrays neighbor love definitively as the practice of mercy. We remember why Jesus tells this parable. He has just given the commandment to love one another. In response, one of the scribes asked Jesus, "Who is my neighbor?"

Jesus responds by telling the parable of the Good Samaritan (Luke 10:25–37). The parable tells the story of a man robbed and left wounded outside the city gates on the road to Jericho. A priest and a scribe each pass him by, rushing to get to their respective appointments. The only one to stop to attend to the man is a Samaritan, a person considered foreign to the Jewish people. The Samaritan treats the man's wounds, takes him to a nearby inn, pays in part for his stay at the inn, and promises to pay the full bill and to take the man with him when he returns.

A close reading of the story reveals that Jesus is offering a very surprising answer to the question. At the beginning of the story we are thinking that the answer to the question "who is my neighbor?" is the man lying wounded on the road. But by the end of the story we are no longer looking at the neighbor who is wounded but rather at the neighbor who is acting. The scribe therefore answers that the neighbor is the one who shows mercy. In the beginning we think the parable is about whom we should assist. But the end is really about who we are called to be. We are called to be like the Good Samaritan—that is, to be a neighbor.

Like the surprising ending, many of us forget that this parable was never primarily a moral one. Many great preachers and theologians see in it the story of our redemption by Christ. For instance, the Venerable Bede (673–735) wrote that the wounded man who lies outside the gates is Adam, wounded by sin, fallen, outside the gates of Eden. The priest and the Levite, representing the tradition and the law, are unable to do anything for Adam. Along comes the Good Samaritan, the Christ, a foreigner, one not from here, who tends to Adam's wounds, takes him to the inn (which is the church), gives a down payment (which is his life) for Adam's healing or salvation, and promises to return for him (the second coming) when he will pay in full for the redemption and take him with him into his kingdom.

The parable then is first and foremost not a story about how we should treat others, but rather the story of what Christ has done for us. We are called to follow the actions of the Good Samaritan not because the parable is an attractive one, but because it is a retelling of the entire Gospel.

The parable is not, then, one among many: it serves as the foundational explanation of the love commandment. As William Spohn notes, it has a privileged position in the Gospels and a privileged position in the church that hears the Gospel proclaimed.[1]

This leads to the second point—namely, that the scriptures name mercy as the condition for salvation. This is made clear in the Last Judgment in Matthew 25 where those are saved because they performed what we later called the corporal works of mercy, which we named above.

The parable of Matthew 25 is striking in that everyone is surprised by the judgment. Let us remember the parable. The King is there and the goats and sheep stand before them. The goats are condemned to hell. "Why?" ask the goats. The King responds, "Because you did not feed me when I was hungry, clothe me when I was naked," and so forth. The goats say, "But when did we see you hungry, or naked?" The King says, "What you did not do for the least, you did not do to me." Similarly the King summons the sheep to enter his Kingdom. "Why?" ask the sheep. The King says, "Because you fed me when I was hungry, clothed me when I was naked," and so forth. "When did we do that?" they ask. And the King answers, "Whenever you did it for the least, you did it to me." Thus, while the sheep never realized that in feeding the hungry they were feeding the King, unfortunately the goats never realized that by not visiting the sick, they were not visiting the Lord.

For the Gospel writers, we will be judged by whether we practiced mercy and we will not be excused if we knew not to practice it. Often the Gospels remind us that we should know that we should be merciful. We saw, for instance, how Jesus contrasted the Good Samaritan with the priest and the scribe who pass by the wounded man. In Luke 16:19–31, Jesus tells the parable of the rich man who steps over and ignores the daily pleas of poor Lazarus, begging at the rich man's gates. When the rich man dies and is sent to Hades, he asks for relief, but the Lord says, "You ignored Lazarus for his whole life." Like the goats, the rich man in Luke 6 learns this "moral" in Hades: he never showed mercy to poor Lazarus begging at his gate. The practice of mercy, whether we know it or not, is the measure of our judgment.

Third, our entire theological tradition is expressed in terms of mercy—that is, the willingness to enter into the chaos of others so as to answer them in their need. Like the Good Samaritan stopping for wounded Adam, attending to someone in need is no simple affair. Helping anyone in need is entering into the entire "problem" or "chaos" of their situation.

Thus, the creation is bringing order out of the chaos of the universe, the incarnation is God's entry into the chaos of human existence, and the redemption is bringing us out of the chaos of our slavery to sin. Christ's own entrance into the chaos of death occasions our hope in the risen life, and his pledge to return again is a pledge to deliver us from the chaos of our own lives. Every action of God is aimed at rescuing us. One of my favorite understandings of God's rescue of us comes from the meditation on the Trinity in the *Spiritual Exercises* of Saint Ignatius. In it, the three persons of the blessed Trinity consider the chaos of the world wherein most people are going to hell. They decide that we must be saved: one of the persons will enter into our lives to keep us from all falling into the abyss of hell, itself pure chaos.

Fourth, early Christianity defined itself by the practice of mercy. We saw earlier that, in *The Rise of Christianity*, Rodney Stark argues that Christianity flourished by the merciful acts of Christians who lived in urban areas marked by "social chaos and chronic urban misery." Moreover, unlike the pagan religions, Christianity was merciful because the God of the Christians commanded mercy.

Stark notes the effect this mercy had on the Roman Empire:

Christianity revitalized life in Greco-Roman cities by providing new norms and new kinds of social relationships able to cope with many urgent urban problems. To cities filled with the homeless and impoverished, Christianity offered charity as well as hope. To cities filled with newcomers and strangers, Christianity offered an immediate basis for attachments. To cities filled with orphans and widows, Christianity provided a new and expanded sense of family.[2]

These four reasons (the paradigm for neighbor love in the Good Samaritan parable, the Gospels' demand for mercy as the condition for our salvation, the writing of our entire theological tradition in the key of mercy, and the actual historical rootedness of our church in the merciful practices of first-century Christians) place mercy in a privileged position for identifying the Roman Catholics as such.

The centrality of the practice of mercy in the moral life of the church cannot be overlooked. It ranks among the activities that best describe the moral life of the church: the confession of sins, obeying the Ten Commandments, developing the virtues, and practicing the corporal and spiritual works of mercy.

Mercy is so important because it is, above all, the experience we have of God. In response to that mercy, we become imitators of the God in whose image we are made. Likewise, in answer to Christ's call to follow him, we practice mercy. Thomas Aquinas asks the question whether mercy is the greatest virtue (II.II.30.4) and responds that charity is the greatest virtue because by it we are united in love to God, but, second to charity, mercy is the greatest because by it we exemplify God in God's actions and, therefore, we become like God.

THE EARLY TRADITION OF THE CORPORAL WORKS OF MERCY

Much could be written about how the corporal works of mercy developed as such. As noted above, today we know the seven that are part of our tradition: feed the hungry, give drink to the thirsty, shelter the homeless, clothe the naked, visit the sick, visit the imprisoned, and bury the dead. These are later paired with the spiritual works: give good counsel, teach the ignorant, admonish sinners, console the afflicted, pardon offenses and injuries, bear offenses patiently, and pray for the living and the dead.

While the first six of the corporal works of mercy are found in the Last Judgment parable in Matthew 25:34–45, it took several centuries for the final articulation of these seven to become a cornerstone of the Christian life. Eventually they paralleled other groups of seven like the sacraments, the deadly sins, and the virtues (the four cardinal—fortitude, temperance, justice, and prudence—and three theological—faith, hope, and love).

Before the set mantra of seven was firmly situated, Christians heard the divine injunction to practice mercy. John never tires of recommending it (e.g., 1 John 4:20–21). Luke tells us how deacons are appointed to serve the most marginalized (Acts 6:1–6). Paul writes to Timothy about the selection of widows who, like the deacons, are to serve those in need (1 Tim. 5:9–10). Collectively and institutionally, the apostolic church promoted the service of mercy.

Almsgiving became an early expression of mercy. In the apostolic age, the practice of the collection began when Paul instructed the Corinthians to set aside a collection for the first day of every week (1 Cor. 16:1–2), presumably during the Eucharist. Later Clement writes: "Almsgiving is good as a penance for sin; fasting is better than prayer, but almsgiving is better than both, and charity covers a multitude of sins" (2 Clem. 16).

These many calls to mercy were heeded. For instance, Cyprian, bishop of Carthage, led his congregation to respond to victims of the plague in 252. Bishop Dionysius provided a narrative of his community's response to the plague in Alexandria in 259: "Most of our brethren, in their surpassing charity and brotherly love did not spare themselves and clinging to one another fearlessly visited the sick and ministered to them. Many, after having nursed and consoled the sick, contracted the illness and cheerfully departed this life. The best of our brethren died in this way, some priests and deacons, and some of the laity" (Eusebius, *History of the Church*, 7.22.9).

Why is the call to mercy made? Normally, six motives are found in the writings of the scriptures and among the fathers. First, Proverbs 15:27 encourages us to practice mercy for the remission of our sins—that is, in gratitude for God's merciful stance toward our sinfulness. John Chrysostom (344?–407) sees mercy here as the queen of the virtues outweighing all our burdensome sins.[3]

Second, Tobit 12:8–9 tells us that for our prayers to be heard by God, works of mercy should accompany them. Several of the fathers (Augustine [354–430], Cyprian [d. 258], Leo the Great [d. 461], and John Chrysostom) preached on this theme.

Third, Matthew 6:20 suggests that works of mercy will lead to eternal reward, a motivation that Augustine often used.

Fourth, Matthew 25:40 reveals to us that any merciful action is for the sake of the Lord. Cyprian called this the most powerful of all motives, and here many of the fathers promoted the figures of Mary of Bethany and Zacchaeus as models of mercy. Similarly, the celebrated episode of Martin of Tours (316?–397) giving his cloak to the beggar became a motif throughout the church.

Fifth, Lactantius (c. 250–c. 325) and Ambrose (340?–397) urge mercy to fortify human solidarity and to extend the circle of fellowship in the Lord. Finally, Clement of Alexandria (d. 215), John Chrysostom, and Leo the Great remind us that works of mercy bring us into the life of perfection; by practicing mercy we become more like the God who entered into our own chaos.

In short, the claim of mercy engages some of the most fundamental interests that Catholics have.

THE PRACTICE OF MERCY IN THE
MIDDLE AGES AND THE RENAISSANCE

In the Middle Ages, the monasteries became centers of the practice of mercy. One account from the famed monastery at Cluny, for instance, informs us that seventeen thousand persons were cared for in one year. Among the Cistercians, every abbey had a guest house for pilgrims, travelers, and the poor. There the abbot waited on them after welcoming them first by prostrating himself at their feet, for in welcoming the guest, the abbot welcomed Christ.

Besides the monks, many pious lay persons participated in the works of mercy by forming associations. These began in Naples in the tenth century and later appeared in Tuscany. By the twelfth century they were throughout France, Spain, and Italy, assisting the religious and mostly establishing and maintaining hospitals. For instance, in 1217 a hospital that once belonged to a religious community was handed over to a corporation of four priests, thirty laymen, and twenty-five laywomen. By the thirteenth and fourteenth century these activities were flourishing throughout Europe.

With the spirit of Francis and Dominic in the thirteenth century, many professional laypersons became inspired and answered with great imagination. For instance, in 1244 the head porter of a wool guild in Florence (Pier Luca Borsi) formed the Company of Mercy with money collected by taxing colleagues for swearing. Others reached out to those suffering from leprosy. The Knights of St. Lazarus established three thousand hospitals for those suffering from the dreaded disease. Later, hospitals for the blind and foundlings for orphans were also founded.

One effect of the Crusades was the widespread practice of prostitution. In their aftermath, foundations were established to provide these women sanctuary; in turn, the women formed religious congregations. In the thirteenth century, for instance, the Congregation of the Penitents of St. Mary Magdalene had thirty communities throughout Europe.

By the sixteenth century, the establishment of guilds, along with the innovations of new religious orders like the Jesuits and the important reforms of the Council of Trent, provided new impetus for laypersons to belong to confraternities. These confraternities wed spiritual devotion with the practice of mercy. They had an enormous influence on the moral formation of Roman Catholics. Here let me mention only two. The Company of Divine Love was established to respond to those with syphilis, which broke out throughout Europe in the mid-1490s. Sufferers from this incurable disease were abandoned by families because of shame and by hospitals for fear of contagion. In 1499, the first hospital for the incurables was built in Genoa, then another in Rome, and others in Naples, Venice, and finally throughout Europe. The one in Rome, at the chapel of St. James on the Via Flaminia, served the needs of the pilgrims. That chapel and its *Hospedale degl' Incurabili* (Hospital for the Incurables) served the needs of those suffering from syphilis. The hospital became one of the most famous of Europe, where a variety of saints, from Camillus to Carlo Borromeo, served.

In 1498, Queen Eleanor of Portugal established the Confraternity of Misericordia. In 1516 it had one hundred members: fifty from the nobility, fifty from the working class, all dedicated to the fourteen works of mercy. By the queen's death in 1525 there were sixty-one branches of the confraternity. From the seventeenth to the nineteenth century, twenty-five confraternities were established in Portuguese colonies. Many still stand today.

ONE WORK: VISITING THE PRISONER

To appreciate the Catholic imagination at work in so many ways through the works of mercy, let us consider just one work: visiting the prisoner. This work has been practiced throughout the life of the church. Inasmuch as they were persecuted, church members visited their imprisoned brothers and sisters and worked to liberate them. Like Tertullian, Cyprian, and others, St. Ignatius of Antioch wrote (in his letter to the Christians of Smyrna), "When the Christians become aware that one of their number is a prisoner and suffering for the name of Christ, they take upon themselves all his needs and, if possible, they free him."

Early Christians routinely sought to comfort their fellow Christians who were imprisoned and sought their blessing as well. No less than Christ had been a prisoner. Thus, like Peter, Paul, and many of the apostles, imprisoned Christians were perceived as not only people in need but also people of courage and holiness. Working to visit, console, and liberate them were in themselves their own reward.

Clement of Rome tells us in his first chapter to the Corinthians that many ransomed others by offering themselves in exchange for the one held hostage.

Later in the twelfth century, a time of enormous spiritual and ecclesial developments, charitable institutions were established for the release of prisoners. The Trinitarians, founded by St. John of Malta, were singularly dedicated to ransoming prisoners and laboring to alleviate the conditions of those who remained in slavery. Similarly, the Order of Mercy was founded by St. Peter Nolasco for the same task.

In another period of spiritual renewal, the sixteenth century, religious orders were founded and their members worked along with other ministries for the care and release of prisoners. The Jesuits, for instance, provided a variety of services. The Jesuit historian John O'Malley reminds us first that these prisoners were either debtors or those awaiting trial, sentencing, or execution. In Rome, for example, over half the imprisoned were debtors from the poorer classes; the others, awaiting trial, had not yet had their guilt established. Jesuits took care of the imprisoned by preaching, catechizing, and confessing the imprisoned, and bringing them food and alms. In Italy and Spain, Jesuits spent a great deal of time raising funds through begging so as to pay off the prisoners' creditors. Elsewhere they begged for money to ransom back prisoners taken by the Turks. Likewise, they preached against slave-taking raids.

Sometimes the Jesuits worked to improve the plight of prisons. In Palermo, for instance, a confraternity was founded based on one Jesuit's work to improve the sanitary conditions of prisoners. Another confraternity organized by the Jesuits, the Confraternity of the Imprisoned, was founded for laypersons in Rome, and it generated other confraternities in six other cities throughout Italy.[4]

Other confraternities of the laity also dedicated themselves to those in prison. In Rome, the Archconfraternity of Charity was specifically for those in captivity, as was the Confraternity of Pietà and Our Lady of Loretto in Milan. In France, confraternities such as the Work of Prisons in Marseilles and the Confraternity of Mercy in Lyons were solely dedicated to prisoners' needs, while the White Penitents and the Sisters of the Dominican Third Order were singularly dedicated to the needs of women prisoners.

Another confraternity, in Florence, was dedicated to prisoners awaiting execution, most of whom were political prisoners. They would visit the prisoners and spend the night with them before the execution, praying with them and helping them to identify with Jesus as a condemned prisoner. The following day, a confraternity member would walk to the gallows with each prisoner, walking ahead of him and holding a painted panel of the suffering Christ in front of his face so that the condemned man could keep his gaze fixed on Jesus instead of on the crowds or the executioners. Six hundred years later, Sister Helen Prejean provides the same support in her accompaniment of those who are sentenced to death for capital crimes: she attends their executions, telling them to look on her face and see the face of Christ. She details her work in her beautiful book, *Dead Man Walking*.[5]

From these experiences of the prisons, there grew subsequently numerous critical voices that protested the conditions and started movements of reform to correct conditions among the imprisoned in Spain, Italy, France, and England.

We cannot underestimate the relevance of these confraternities: hundreds of them took care of prisoners and captives; others were established for the care of the mentally ill as well as those who are unable to hear and/or speak. These confraternities are only paralleled by the extraordinary number of religious orders that themselves adopt a work of mercy to identify with its own charism.

I too am involved in prison ministry. Sister Maureen Clark, C.S.J., has been working in prison ministry for many years and currently visits, supports, listens to, and works with the women at the women's correctional facility in Framingham, Massachusetts. Several years ago, Maureen was looking for new clergy to preside at Sunday mass and one of her volunteer musicians, at that time a doctoral student of mine, promptly volunteered me.

My schedule is busy. But I decided that I wanted to go. Having grown up as the son of a New York City police detective, prisons have always been frightening places for me. They became more terrifying when my dad, who later was involved in the investigation of the Attica uprising, took me through that prison. As I walked through the cavernous, gray hallways, I became afraid that, by some accident, I would be left "inside."

Years later, while visiting a Jesuit friend in southern California, he informed me that we were going to Tijuana to say mass in the city jail. He told me that this was the happiest task of his priestly ministry. He described the place as very confining and very chaotic, and did not hesitate to let me know about the broad diversity of crimes for which these men were detained, from petty debts to kidnapping and murder. I remember entering the cell with all the fear of a young child, watching my friend greet, embrace, and chat with the mingling prisoners, while I rigidly stood by the makeshift altar, occasionally glancing (almost frantically) at the guards on the other side of the common area. The strongest memory I have of that place is that when the liturgy was over, the guards announced that they could not open the gates to let us out for another twenty to thirty minutes. My friend smiled, shrugged his shoulders, and went back to the prisoners. I stayed by the doors and waited. I was convinced I had been left "inside."

The invitation from Sister Maureen to come to Framingham was not, then, what I would have put on my annual wish list. Yet, in light of the many fears that I have had to face, I thought, why not this one? The situation would be different, after all. I would be in Framingham, not Tijuana or Attica.

I arrived and met Sister Maureen and about twenty volunteers who were among a group of about one hundred who take turns coming to the Sunday evening mass. They led me through the procedures. I had to leave my wallet, wristwatch, car keys, and cash in the lockers. I had to sign in. I had to wait (nearly an hour). I was searched. I was eventually allowed to pass through innumerable gates and doors to go to the room where the mass would be held.

The mass was extraordinarily consoling. The women were welcoming. Several hundred showed up. They set up the altar, checked the readings, joined the choir, or just sat and prayed. They wanted to pray, especially for their children and, yes, grandchildren as well as for their sister inmates. Their prayers were many. They enjoyed the liturgy.

But they were in prison and whatever personal freedom I had gained by facing my fear, I realized that their freedom was incredibly restricted. I especially understood this when one prayed for another younger woman who had a hearing the next day. The hearing was to determine whether she would be released earlier. There was an evident but quiet desperation on the faces of many as the prayer was uttered.

"Do you like this work?" I later asked Maureen. "I love these women," she answered.

Practicing Mercy Today

Today many persons speak of an emerging lay ministry. But during a variety of periods in the church's life, laypersons—animated both by their own God-given talents and by the fundamental experience of God's mercy—were ministers. Their legacy of leadership and service needs to be studied, for it was phenomenal. A proper place to find it is in the variety of associations and confraternities in both the medieval and Renaissance periods. In those times of spiritual richness and economic prosperity, times like our own, the laity, alongside clergy and religious, imitated the merciful ways of the Good Samaritan.

But we can think of more recent examples. Here the Society of St. Vincent de Paul easily comes to mind. Comprised originally of six students in Paris in 1833, the group's founder, A. Frederic Ozanam (1813–1853), recognized the call to relieve need but also to address the cause of the need. For this reason he identified two virtues for the society: the call of charity and of justice. Today, many recognize in his writings on social justice an anticipation of the social encyclical *Rerum Novarum*.

Ozanam's society eventually expanded throughout the world. For instance, in 1845, a group of lay Catholics met in St. Louis and formed the first council in the United States. The society has grown to the point where it now numbers some six hundred thousand members worldwide and has a presence in 132 countries.

In other instances, the laity and the religious often collaborate on a variety of corporal works of mercy, and these works are much more institutional, with central administrations designed to service effectively the needs of those in chaos. If we look at health care in the United States today, we see about 13 percent of all hospital beds belonging to Catholic health care institutions. The Catholic Church is, therefore, the largest singular health care provider in the United States.

These health care centers were almost all founded by religious women. Their distinctive spiritualities grew into a legacy of care, adaptation, responsiveness, and inventiveness that continues to be active today. Still, with shifts in understanding the nature of religious life, many Catholics are opting to serve the church not in religious life, but as laypersons. With diminishing numbers in their ranks, these religious orders are looking at a variety of ways of guaranteeing the future of their apostolic institutions while promoting their original charism. In a way, they are handing on to another population the ministry that they so ably led. Better, they are incorporating into their own original vision a partnership with others.

One example of such innovation is Catholic Health Initiatives (CHI). Their mission "is to nurture the healing ministry of the Church by bringing it new life, energy, and viability in the twenty-first century. Fidelity to the Gospel urges us to emphasize human dignity and social

justice as we move toward the creation of healthier communities."
A national not-for-profit health care organization, it is composed of
sixty-three hospitals and forty-three long-term care, assisted-living,
independent-living, and residential facilities. Its ministry is found in
nineteen states. They serve sixty-four rural and urban communities
and represent more than sixty-seven thousand employees.

Multiple congregations entered into a partnership that, in turn,
engaged lay leaders as well and formed a system that models the
future of ministry: a truly equal religious-lay partnership. Because of
their commitment to promoting new models of health care ministry,
the hallmark of CHI is their mission and ministry fund. This assists
projects described as "collaborative," "innovative," and "transferable"
that aim to address the root causes of illness in any of the communities they serve. Generating new offspring, CHI seeks to continue in
a ministry that has always been known for its inventiveness and its
responsiveness.

Whatever corporal work of mercy we think of, invariably we
find its contemporary expression. If we were to think of sheltering
the homeless, we can think of the forty-five million refugees and dis-
placed persons around the world. Within that enormous population,
80 percent are women and children. Catholic Relief Services, together
with Caritas Internationalis, dedicate themselves to the diverse needs
of these people. If we think of teenage runaways, Covenant House
alone served over fifty thousand youth last year.

Many are, like the hospitals and social services, simply Roman
Catholic in identity. Others are predominantly Christian, like Bread
for the World, or without any religious affiliation, like Amnesty International. But in each instance, these associations have a core mission; they often provide direct service, but also political advocacy in
an attempt to get the social welfare states to respond to the citizens'
needs. But the wisdom that their forerunners provide—in whatever
work it was—continues to shape the practical agendas that these
agencies pursue today.

People from all walks of life seek to enter into the chaos of another in a variety of ways. Despite this, the long legacy of religious orders, diocesan programs, lay associations, and confraternities has deeply embedded in the Roman Catholic tradition its distinctive trademark that promotes mercy above all practical virtues.

MERCY OR JUSTICE

Sometimes people get concerned that mercy means helping a person out, but justice means working for the structural changes that so often oppress people. Mercy, people fear, is temporary action and doesn't move for social change. But this chapter shows us otherwise. By getting involved in mercy, people understand why others are in chaos.

Mercy calls us to meet human beings in need. By meeting them, often we realize that their situation is compromised. We go to a prison—we realize the need for prison reform; we visit the homeless—we need to develop shelters. We go to the shelters, and we realize the shelters need to be changed, and so on.

In the real merciful engagement we realize that by entering into the chaos of others, we eventually have to face what causes that chaos. But usually we cannot know about those needs until we have a merciful engagement first.

I think people who work for justice without knowing and meeting those who are suffering often have presumptions for action that are not helpful. I think that acting from mercy allows us to meet people in need and in turn we are moved to justice. But beginning with justice, without first having a merciful encounter, strikes me as very uninformed.

I have watched students here at Boston College enter many different immersion programs. In most instances, in that merciful meeting with people who are suffering, students return convinced that they need somehow to choose a professional field that will serve the cause of advocacy and justice. Mercy leads them to justice. By encountering the other, they are able to be awakened to the call of justice.

STUDY QUESTIONS

Do you think there are other more important issues that define us as Catholic, other than mercy?

I define mercy as the willingness to enter into the chaos of another. Do you agree with that?

How do you act mercifully without being condescending?

What works of mercy do you think are more appropriate for today's contemporary world?

Chapter Eight

CULTIVATING THE
CARDINAL VIRTUES

IN ORDER TO THINK ABOUT VIRTUE, LET US CONSIDER ONE OF THE chief proponents of the cardinal virtues—Thomas Aquinas. This great Renaissance theologian is an important resource from the tradition, and to appreciate him, we must consider not only his work, but his life and his context.

Yet, to appreciate the exceptional importance of the medieval Scholastics in general and the thirteenth-century *Summa Theologiae* of Thomas Aquinas in particular, we have to turn first to the work of twelfth-century ascetical theology that made possible Thomas's great work.

THE IMPORTANCE OF TWELFTH-CENTURY ASCETICAL THEOLOGY

We saw in the introductory chapter that, with few exceptions, the subject of moral theology was basically for assisting monks and priests to be good confessors. The penitentials, the confessional manuals, and the later moral manuals with their singular focus on sin were specifically distinguished from works of ascetical, spiritual, or devotional theology, which were about the pursuit of "perfection" or growing in the life of discipleship. If we recall the first principle of the natural law—that is, to avoid evil and to pursue the good—then moral theology was singularly concerned with the avoidance of evil and ascetical theology was about pursuing the good.

When we think of the history of ascetical theology,[1] we must inevitably turn to the twelfth century. "The twelfth century has long been seen as a turning point in the history of Latin spirituality," claims the great historian of Western spirituality, Bernard McGinn. "[T]here can be no argument that the twelfth century was fascinated with the mystery of the human person as *imago Dei.*" Through the spiritual friendship of Aelred of Rievaulx (1109–1167), the insistence on conscience by Abelard (1079–1142), the location of the image of God in human freedom by Bernard of Clairvaux (1090–1153), the knowledge of the way of the Lord and the appreciation of the goodness of the human body and the delight of the passions by Hildegard of Bingen (1098–1179), and the understanding of the interpersonal human subject as in the image of the three-personed God by Richard of St. Victor (1123–1173), the theologians of the twelfth century developed a powerful, relational understanding of the human as a foundation for their spirituality.[2]

Another great historian, Caroline Walker Bynum, agrees with McGinn: "No period was ever busier creating structures for its piety than the twelfth century."[3] Like McGinn, Bynum studies Bernard of Clairvaux, who with "other 'new monks' stressed discovery of self—and of self-love—as the first step in a long process of returning to the love and likeness of God, a love and likeness in which the individual is not dissolved into God but rather becomes God's partner and friend."[4] Bernard's spirituality as well as his contemporaries' drew deeply from the scriptures and cultivated in a particular way a devotion to the humanity of Jesus, which moved readers into greater intimacy with Jesus and with those who shared the devotion.[5] In developing a highly relational vision of the human, the twelfth century never compromised the person and in fact discovered "the self, the inner mystery, the inner man, the inner landscape."[6]

The discovery of the self did not mean, however, an endorsement of individualism; as Bynum argues, the twelfth century "also discovered the group in two very precise senses: it discovered that many separate 'callings' or 'lives' were possible in the church, and it elaborated a language for talking about how individuals became a part of them (the language of 'conforming to a model')."[7]

These various twelfth-century charismatic persons, who discovered not only the "person" but also the "group," were the forerunners of the great religious orders founded in the thirteenth century. In fact, in many ways, their appreciation of humanity as being in the image of the Trinity—that is, as being in the image of the triune God—becomes the foundation of the entire Renaissance.

I first tasted the Renaissance in 1981 by studying Italian in Florence so as to prepare for doctoral studies in Rome. I went there with a wonderful guide, my friend the historian John O'Malley. I remember when we first entered that incredible art collection in the Uffizi Gallery. There, in the very first room, I saw the birth of the Renaissance: three enormous canvases of the Madonna enthroned surrounded by angels presenting the Godhead in the human person of her infant son, Jesus. Here was the glory of God in the human fully alive and here were Duccio, Cimabue, and Giotto presenting their masterpieces. In the birth of Jesus, the Renaissance celebrated humanity.

Into that world, Dominic, Francis, and Clare entered preaching the Gospel. Previously, those who sought to be disciples of Christ in the pursuit of "perfection," as it would be called, chose the monastery outside of any urban place. But Dominic, Francis, and Clare changed religious history by leaving the isolated monastic model to pursue the evangelization of the vibrant economic and political urban centers of Europe.

THOMAS AQUINAS

In 1224, seven years after Dominic received papal approbation for the founding of the Order of Preachers, Thomas Aquinas was born in a little town (Roccasecca, "Dry Rock" in English) in southern Italy.[8] At the age of six, Thomas's politically ambitious parents sent him to the famous Benedictine Abbey, Monte Cassino, expecting, even then, that he would eventually become abbot. The appointment would secure one of the most significant ecclesiastical titles of thirteenth-century central Italy. At fifteen, however, Thomas left the Benedictine community and, after five years of studies in Naples, he entered the relatively new order of St. Dominic.

Thomas entered the Dominicans because of their work in the towns, their promotion of the Gospel, their vow of evangelical poverty, and their newness. His family was not happy with his decision to abandon Monte Cassino for the sake of evangelical poverty. Under orders from their widowed mother, his brothers kidnapped him and held him in house detention for a year (apparently a rather frequent parental practice, considering that Francis of Assisi himself suffered the same fate). When his family relented and released him, the Dominicans made the astute decision to send Thomas away from Naples to Paris for three years of studies (1245–1248) and another four in Cologne (1248–1252). In 1252 he returned to Paris and taught his first major work, the *Commentary on the Sentences of Peter Lombard*, and then assumed the position of regent master for the Dominicans at the University of Paris. There in Paris he finished *De veritate*, began the *Summa Contra Gentiles*, and lectured on the Gospel of Saint Matthew. After a brief stay in Naples (1260–1261), he went to the papal town of Orvieto for four years, where he completed the *Contra Gentiles* and his commentary on the book of Job, among other works. In 1265, he began his teaching at Rome, where he remained for three years before being summoned to return to Paris for an extraordinary second term of teaching. As we shall see, these seven years in Rome and Paris were remarkable. In 1272, he left Paris and returned to Naples for two years before he died in 1274.

Despite his girth, he was an active man. In fact, Thomas was one of history's major walkers: from Naples to Paris, Paris to Cologne, Cologne to Paris, Paris to Naples, Naples to Orvieto and then to Rome, back to Paris, and back to Naples. Not surprisingly, he collapsed while walking to the Council of Lyons. His death a few days later is ironic: the forty-nine-year-old who abandoned a vocation of Benedictine stability for the more innovative Dominican order died not in his community, but as an infirmed guest in a monastic community not far from Roccasecca and Monte Cassino.

To appreciate the specific contribution of the *Summa Theologiae*, we need to remember that four years after the founding of the Order of Preachers, Pope Innocent III gave all members in the church the requirement to confess their sins once a year just before Easter and he specifically mandated the Dominicans to hear confessions. In response to this new apostolic charge, a few Dominicans wrote a set of confessional manuals describing sins and their gravity. These manuals became the major theological texts that most Dominicans studied. For the most part, the theological formation of Dominicans both in their early stages of life in the community as well as in their ongoing formation later in life was almost exclusively a study of the parsing of sin and its penances as found in the confessional manuals. The exception was for a few extraordinary Dominican students, like Albert, Thomas, and others, who were singled out and sent to one of the *studia*, or study centers, set up at the five major universities of Oxford, Bologna, Paris, Montpelier, and Cologne.

After being a regent master at the study center in Paris, Thomas returned to Italy and attended the provincial chapter at Anagni in the early 1260s. There he proposed an experimental study center for young Dominican students, not among the elite at the universities, but intelligent enough for something more theologically sophisticated than the confessional manuals.[9] The chapter established an experimental personal study center for Thomas at Rome, where eventually he began producing the *Summa Theologiae* for these above-average Dominican students who were open to experiments in a new order.

Thomas wrote the *Summa*, therefore, for very young men with no philosophical background but with intellectual promise. As he wrote in the preface, it was a work for "beginners." (I often think of this experiment as a forerunner of divinity schools like my own Weston Jesuit School of Theology, where we train men and women fairly sophisticated academic theology for either priestly or lay ministry, and not predominantly for doctoral work.)

Thomas divided the *Summa Theologiae* into three parts, with the second part having two sections. The first part is about God's relationship to us as Creator and Mover. The second part is about our response to God; the first section concerns general matters in morals, and the second treats specific virtues, vices, and sins. The third part is about Jesus Christ and the sacraments.

Thomas believed that theology should be dialogical. Nowhere is Thomas more dialogical than in this structure of the *Summa* itself. Consider the three parts: God's divine call in the first; our human response in the second; Jesus, the Word Incarnate, the indwelling of the human in the divine, and the sacraments that mediate his grace in the third. The entire work reflects a dialogue.

Each part is divided into questions and each question is divided into articles. Each article begins in the form of a question and, prior to giving an answer, we find a series of considerations from every kind of author who had ever written on the topic so as to extend the dialogue into one that includes these diverse writers. Thomas's own response to the article's question followed these considerations, and then he answered each of the points of consideration in light of his own response. Through each article Thomas invited the reader into deeper reflection, and so, before moving onto another topic, Thomas proceeded instead to another article that immediately flowed from the previous answer given. These related articles become stages of a descent into the depths of inquiry first posed by the original question.

When Thomas exhausted one question, he moved onto the next. All along the inquiring intellect of Thomas engaged the reader. There are over two thousand articles in the *Summa* and through them we learn that the *Summa* is less a work of theological opinion and more a method of theological investigation.[10]

Like his work, Thomas's life was a dialogue as well. For instance, from 1269 to 1272, during his second tenure in Paris, Thomas had four scribes to whom he simultaneously (it seems) dictated—to one, the *Summa Theologiae*; to another, his commentaries on Aristotle's works (e.g., *Ethics*, *Metaphysics*, *Physics*); to another, his commentaries on the scriptures (specifically, John's Gospel and the Pauline Epistles); and to the fourth, the polemical discourses against the anti-mendicants (opponents of the newly founded Dominican and Franciscan orders) and the Averroists (the followers of Ibn Rochd [1126–1198], an Arabian philosopher who believed in the independence of philosophy from revelation).

In light of this portrait, the typical iconography of Thomas as a somewhat large but silent figure is peculiar. The man who left Monte Cassino was rarely, except in his last months, speechless. On the contrary, he was lecturing, debating, commenting, discoursing, and dictating with great relish. Moreover, one semiannual university event that he enjoyed was the Quodlibetales (in English, the "whatevers"). These sessions occurred during Advent and Lent when the entire university was assembled and random questions from the audience were submitted, dealing with whatever topic the questioner asked. While Thomas commented on the Trinity, he was also answering questions about whether one can enjoy long, warm baths.

Thomas, the man who joined the Order of Preachers, loved the Word. His theology and his life, therefore, were dialogical. His use of so many sources and his variety of interests demonstrate how convincingly he believed in the gift of human reason. No wonder, then, that he asserted that the human is made in God's image by being rational.

Through the *Summa*, then, Thomas did not only leave the reader with new insights; more important, he prompted the reader to emulate the probing intellect that wrote it. Thomas drew us into the habit of inquiring deeply.

Thomas was, of course, committed to the notion of rationality as deeply human and personal. Like other medieval Scholastics from the twelfth through the sixteenth century, Thomas investigated ways of expressing faith through reason. Inasmuch as theology was seen as a science investigating God and the human, morality specifically studied humanity as responding lovingly to the initiative of God.

This study was then highly anthropological and naturally depended on the virtues to outline an appropriate moral identity for the Christian. Virtue became then the key way that Renaissance theologians like Thomas developed their moral theology. Like everyone else in the Renaissance, Thomas was more concerned with the human being than with human action.

In the preface to the second section of the second part of the *Summa Theologiae*, Thomas wrote that all of morals comes down to the virtues. Not only did he dedicate the whole second part of the *Summa* to the virtues, but while at Paris for the second time he wrote his commentary on the *Ethics of Aristotle* (1271) as well as his works on ordinary virtues, charity, hope, and the cardinal virtues (*De virtutibus in communi, De caritate, De spe*, and *De virtutibus cardinalibus*, 1269–1272). His ethical reflection singularly revolved around the virtues.

I cannot in any adequate way summarize Thomas's work on the virtues, but I can underline certain key factors. Let me name here three. First, Thomas believed that every human action is a moral action. In order to appreciate the significance of this claim, I suggest you take an imaginary piece of paper and write down five moral matters. Did you include war, abortion, homosexuality, AIDS, racism? Probably. Probably you wrote down big issues that have great social claims on all of us. But now turn the imaginary paper over and write down five concerns with which you woke up this morning. Did those concerns include repairing a relationship; drinking less; eating less; getting more sleep; doing more work or getting more leisure; talking with your spouse, children, or boss; being less compulsive or obsessive; being less timid; being more assertive; confronting a friend; supporting a friend; being more generous? This side of the paper, I suggest, is also moral matter. Ordinary life is the matter for moral reflection, intention, and action.

When Thomas asked whether there are any actions that are free of moral meaning, he responded that if we are talking about actions in the abstract, then there are indifferent actions. Once we discuss actions that we do, however, then the only actions that are indifferent are those that we do unconsciously. He gives an example: "Stroking one's beard, unknowingly." Otherwise, everything else is about moral living. Even small actions? Yes, Thomas replies, and uses the scriptures to talk about an incidental act like breaking stalks of grain in a field.

Second, Thomas believed that we become what we do. What does this mean? Thomas appreciated that anything that we intentionally do (and he always meant intentionality in the broad sense) makes us become what we are doing. If we were rude in getting to work this morning, we are becoming more rude people. If we were able to laugh at some problems that affected us today, we are developing a sense of humor. If we stopped to help a person in need, we are growing in compassion; if we did not, we are becoming more callous.

Thomas recognized that just as we become what we do, conversely, if we only plan to act, but never realize that action, then we never realize what we can become. If I intend to speak up to my domineering boss, but never do, I will never attain the assertive stance that I believe is necessary. If I intend to give up drinking large quantities of beer, but never do, I will continue to be a heavy drinker.

Third, Thomas argued that each person ought to establish a proactive agenda. If we become what we do, then we should intend ways of acting that can shape us better into being the type of people we think we should become. Who, then, should we become? According to Thomas, we should become just, temperate, fortitudinous or steadfast, and prudent people. That is, we should acquire the cardinal virtues, which Thomas acknowledges was the position of Ambrose, Gregory, Cicero, and Augustine.

THE TRADITIONAL CARDINAL VIRTUES

The virtues are called "cardinal" from the Latin word *cardo*, which means "hinge." They are cardinal because they are "principal" in that they are fundamental hinges on which hangs our image of the moral person. Thomas wrote that these four virtues rightly order all our appetitive and intellectual powers that enable us to act: prudence orders our practical reason; justice orders the will, or our intellectual appetite; temperance and fortitude order the passions, which are divided into the concupiscible—desiring power—and the irascible—struggling power—respectively. The four virtues are cardinal because they sufficiently order all the components within us that are engaged in moral acting.[11]

In a manner of speaking, Thomas's cardinal virtues are really two. With Aristotle, Aquinas upheld the absolute priority of prudence. No cardinal virtue is more important. Prudence, of course, is not that tepid little virtue that warns us against taking bold steps. On the contrary, prudence is the virtue that looks forward to the overall end of life and sets all subsequent agendas for attaining that end and all intermediate ends. Prudence discerns and sets the standards for the pursuit of the end and therein helps us to articulate the norms of moral action. Moreover, prudence enjoys nearly the same function and authority over the moral virtues that charity does with the infused virtues: as charity unites the infused virtues, prudence unites and connects the moral virtues. In short, the "whole matter of moral virtues falls under the one rule of prudence" (I.II.65.1.ad3).

With what is prudence concerned? Clearly, justice. Aquinas argued that justice governs all our actions. Though the virtues of temperance and fortitude order us interiorly, justice orders all our operations or exterior actions. In a word, when we are just, we are doing things right. The virtues of temperance and fortitude are, then, auxiliaries for justice: we acquire these virtues that order our interior life for the sake of being just and doing justice. Thus, in any moral situation the prudent person asks one central question: "What is the just person to do?" In a manner of speaking, Thomas basically is asking each of us to become just people—that is, people who become, by their just actions, more and more just.[12]

PROPOSING NEW CARDINAL VIRTUES

I would like to take Thomas's cardinal virtues and suggest that for today we need to reform them somewhat. I do this reform by keeping prudence and justice and adding two other virtues that, like justice, are ends in themselves.[13] That is, I agree that temperance and fortitude are auxiliary or helping virtues and that therefore they are not really cardinal virtues.

Why do I not just let matters be? If the cardinal virtues were good enough for Cicero, Augustine, and Thomas, why can they not be sufficient for us?

I see three major reasons. First, contemporary theologians and philosophers repeatedly express dissatisfaction about the sufficiency of justice. They note that morality asks of us more than being just. For instance, my friend Marilyn Martone, a moral theologian at New York's St. John's University, reminds us that many of the twentieth century's most important advocates for justice had a variety of marital difficulties. Is not fidelity a moral virtue, and what happens when the particular obligations of marriage take one away from a more general call for justice?

For this reason, many offer hyphenated phrases, the most famous being "love-justice," which attempts to acknowledge that while working for justice—that is, the equality for all persons—we still need to maintain partial, loving relationships that must be nurtured and sustained. I find the hyphen distracting, however. We are not talking about one virtue, but in fact two distinct and sometimes opposing virtues, justice and love (or fidelity, as I and others prefer to call it).[14] For instance, many family members discover that other family members have a variety of unjust biases, but often they do not relinquish their family ties over the bias. In fact, sometimes rather than falling into perpetual dispute, one might not object to an unjust remark simply because such an objection neither improves the fidelity of the familial relationship nor diminishes the unjust bias of the family member. Or sometimes a friend might stand with another friend who is hurting after isolating him- or herself by expressing bigoted remarks. The friend recognizes the bigotry but might feel that some support is also due. Keeping alive the tension in moral theory seems then to validate the prudential recognition of the tension as it frequently arises in ordinary life.

Second, moral theologians today insist that moral dilemmas are not based on the simple opposition of good and evil but, more frequently, on the clash of goods. Thus we recognize that we cannot possibly imagine justice alone as adequate. We need a framework that raises up the possibility of other goods or cardinal virtues, like fidelity, that in the real world could conflict with one another.

Third, today we believe that the task of moral development is not for an individual to perfect her or his powers, but rather for a person to realize rightly the variety of ways that we are relational. That is, as in the way we started this discussion, we realize as they did in the twelfth century that in the image of the triune God we can only understand ourselves as relational. Therefore virtues do not realize so much interior dispositions as much as they help us to grow in the different ways that we are in relationships.

I propose, then, that the cardinal virtues are the hinges upon which depend the ways we are relational. Our identity is relational in three ways: generally, specifically, and uniquely. Each of these relational ways of being demands a cardinal virtue: as a relational being in general, we are called to justice; as a relational being specifically, we are called to fidelity; as a relational being uniquely, we are called to self-care. These three virtues are cardinal. They have equally urgent claims and they should be pursued as ends in themselves. We are not called to be faithful and self-caring in order to be just, nor are we called to be self-caring and just in order to be faithful. None is auxiliary to the others. They are cardinal. The fourth cardinal virtue is prudence, which determines what constitutes the just, faithful, and self-caring way of living, intending, and acting in the ordinary life.

Our relationality generally is directed to an ordered appreciation for the common good in which we treat all people as equal. As members of the human race, we are expected to respond to all members in general equally and impartially. That is, regardless of our familiarity with a person and regardless of our degree of attraction or repulsion to another, in justice we believe that each person is accorded the same basic fair treatment.

If justice urges us to treat all people equally, then fidelity makes very different claims. Fidelity is the virtue that nurtures and sustains the bonds of those special relationships that humans enjoy whether by blood, marriage, love, citizenship, or sacrament. If justice rests on impartiality and universality, then fidelity rests on partiality and particularity. If justice warns us against favoritism, fidelity asks us to cultivate particular relationships.

Fidelity here is like love in the "just-love" dialectic. Fidelity also addresses the claim that Carol Gilligan made in her important work, *In a Different Voice*.[15] Gilligan criticized Lawrence Kohlberg for arguing that full moral development was found in the person who could reason well about justice as impartial and universal. She countered that the human must aim both for the impartiality of justice as well as the development of particular faithful, partial bonds.

Neither of these virtues, however, addresses the unique relationship that one has with oneself. Care for self enjoys a considered role in our tradition, as, for instance, the command to love God and one's neighbor as oneself. In his writings on the order of charity, Thomas Aquinas, among others, developed this self-love at length.[16] I consider the most important task of self-care to be the formation of one's own conscience, for in that we respond to the God who calls us.

Finally, prudence has the task of integrating the three virtues into our relationships, just as it did when it was among the classical list of the cardinal virtues. Thus, prudence is always vigilantly looking to the future, trying not only to realize the claims of justice, fidelity, and self-care in the here and now, but also calling us to anticipate occasions when each of these virtues can be more fully and integratively acquired. In this way prudence is clearly a virtue that pursues ends and effectively establishes the moral agenda for the person growing in these virtues. But these ends are not really in opposition to, or in isolation from, one another. Rather, prudence helps each virtue to shape its end as more inclusive of the other two.

I also propose that all persons in every culture are constituted by these three ways of being related. I do not mean, however, that these virtues are the same everywhere. Rather the very basics or the skeleton of these virtues is present in every society. Therefore, every culture recognizes that we must respect without any partiality every person as a human being. Every culture also imposes on individuals the obligation to maintain their specific relationships to parents, children, spouse, family members, colleagues, friends, and co-citizens. A variety of loyalties call you and me to uphold the ways we are partial. Finally, every culture calls us to be responsible for our own personal well-being. Thus, wherever we are, these virtues call us to develop the three ways that each person is fundamentally relational.

Furthermore, in every culture, parents train their children in a variety of practices that help their children understand each of these virtues. Parents in New York, Nairobi, Karachi, Manila, Bogota, and Rome teach their children to respect human beings everywhere and that one should treat all persons with justice. Parents also teach their children to have a special regard for their family members. They teach them that their relatives, friends, and classmates are special and that they have particular obligations to them. Parents also teach their children to take care of themselves: to brush their teeth, to get good sleep, to study hard, to dream. Finally, parents help their children figure out ways to attain their goals. They continually mentor their children to appreciate the complexity of prudently assuming the governance of one's life. Parents patiently and consistently listen to their children to find out what they are looking for, what friendships they are wanting to develop, what projects they wish to complete, what dreams they want to realize. Parents everywhere try to help their children develop these four particular virtues: justice, fidelity, self-care, and prudence.

Though every culture proposes these three ways as necessary, every culture promotes justice, fidelity, and self-care differently. Thus these cardinal virtues do not purport to offer a picture of the ideal person, or to exhaust the entire domain of virtue. Rather than being the last word on virtue, they are the first, providing the bare essentials for right human living and specific action. As hinges, the cardinal virtues provide a skeleton of what human persons should basically be.

This skeleton gets filled out in the theater. In the very first moral drama, *Antigone*, we find the heroine perplexed over her moral dilemma. Her brothers have been involved in a great civil war and have thrown all Thebes into chaos. They have killed one another and the new ruler, Creon, determines that Thebans must turn away from the civil war. He rules that the unburied must remain unburied. Antigone thinks nothing of the call to impartiality. She thinks nothing of the ordinary people of Thebes. She only thinks of her brother Polyneices, who remains unburied outside the walls. She wants to be faithful to her brother even if it means Thebes will fall into civil war again and that she will be executed for burying her brother. Her sister Ismene arrives, thinking, well, only of herself. Her moral argument is simply "Antigone, don't do it. Our parents are dead, our brothers were fratricidal, and I only have you. If you bury him, I am without kin." The drama is riveting because it pulls us in each of the three different directions. And the reason we are so pulled is because none of the three main agents has exhibited any prudence—that is, none shows any sense of incorporating the claims of the other two virtues into their agenda.

But if you want something more contemporary and less sophisticated than *Antigone*, then see *Terminator 2*. There, a cyborg (played by Arnold Schwarzenegger) is sent to help a young boy save the world. The boy, however, is more caught up in trying to save his mother, and when forced to choose between saving seven billion humans or his mother, his sense of fidelity trumps his sense of justice. His mother, on the other hand, without any sense of self-care, insists that her son save the world. And we are sure that even after the boy saves both the world and his mother, Arnold will save the boy. Hollywood, unlike ancient Greece, never leaves us with unresolved tension.

MERCY IS WHAT MAKES THE CARDINAL VIRTUES CATHOLIC

We can say that every society enjoys these cardinal virtues but that these virtues are "thin" descriptions of the basic outline of what it means to be moral. If these virtues are "thin" when we speak of them across all the cultures of the world, then it is in specific cultures that these virtues "thicken."[17] Many philosophers and theologians, while recognizing that there are fundamental interests that all human beings share, also acknowledge the influence of local culture and therefore use this distinction between thin and thick. That is, they insist on universal though modest ways of describing basic concerns or ways of being related that are attributable to all human beings no matter where they live.[18] I am one such theologian in my "skeletal" description of how the four cardinal virtues exist in every society. I base that on the two-fold premise that persons of every society are related in three fundamentally distinct ways (impartially, partially, and uniquely) and that everyone needs prudence to govern and integrate these ways.

We call these universal assertions "thin" ones, and from various cultures we seek to "thicken" them. For instance, some understanding of justice (the willingness to be impartial and to give to each her or his due) is presumably present in every culture. Justice in the United States, however, is affected considerably by the American esteem of personal autonomy and its respect of personal rights. Autonomy thickens justice inasmuch as we would not give "the due" to any persons without their consent. Our health care system, for instance, so powerfully protects the rights of the individual that we could not imagine justice in a health care system that did not privilege informed consent. This American understanding of justice differentiates itself from justice in the Philippines, where an emphasis on "smooth interpersonal relationships" governs most social relationships.

Similarly, through autonomy, American understandings of fidelity depend on the importance of mutual consent. In the Philippines, its strong emphasis on cohesion, unity, and peace clearly provides the yeast for translating fidelity into ordinary life.

Cultures give flesh to the skeletal cardinal virtues. This thickening differentiates, then, one virtue in one culture from a similar one in another. Justice, fidelity, and self-care in a Buddhist culture have somewhat similar and somewhat different meanings than they do in a liberal or Confucian context.[19]

From the beginning of this book I have argued that mercy is the trademark of Catholicism. In Catholic cultures, mercy thickens our understanding of the virtues. Inasmuch as mercy is the willingness to enter into the chaos of another so as to respond to the other, mercy thickens justice by taking into account the chaos of the most marginalized. Mercy does not temper justice, as so many believe; rather, mercy prompts us to see that justice applies to all, especially those most frequently without justice, those abandoned to the chaos of the margins. In Catholic cultures, mercy prompts justice to find the neglected, the persecuted, the oppressed, and to bring them into the solidarity of humanity by assisting them in the pursuit of their rights.

Similarly, fidelity in the many relationships we enjoy is enfleshed by mercy. Mercy helps Catholics to see from the start that no relationship is without its chaos and that every relationship requires the merciful practice of reconciliation. In Catholic marriages, for instance, the balm of mercy prompts spouses to enter one another's chaos and to forgive each other not once or twice but seventy times seven times.

Finally, the Catholic practice of self-care urges each person, through mercy, to enter into the deep chaos of one's own distinctively complicated life. By the examination of conscience we believe that the loving, merciful light of Christ illuminates every dimension of the soul and helps us to see what we need to do in the care of ourselves.

In the quest to grow as integrated, constitutively relational disciples of Christ, Catholics look to mercy to translate into practices the cardinal virtues that we all share.

Study Questions

How would you define virtue?

Do you think of a virtuous person as kind of nerdy? Or do you think of a virtuous person as brave, just, sensitive, articulate? Why?

What virtues do you most want to cultivate? Why?

How can a university promote virtue?

PART III

THE FUTURE

Chapter Nine

HOPE AND LEADERSHIP

IN LIGHT OF THE CHURCH'S CRISIS AT THE BEGINNING OF THE third millennium, many turn to virtues like integrity, honesty, humility, trustworthiness, and prudence to launch discussions about fundamental qualities for good leadership. I argue here, in ten points, that hope, a frequently overlooked virtue, provides a worthy training ground for becoming both the type of leaders the church needs as well as the type of people who live with moral wisdom.

First, hope is the theological virtue that, according to Thomas Aquinas, resolutely pursues the end, which is God, who is love (II. II.17.1). As such, hope is particularly applicable to the ambiguous time in which Christians live, that "already but not yet." The time of our redemption by Christ is already here, but the time of our fulfillment in the kingdom of God is not yet.

The Christian tradition accords an extraordinary privilege to hope and the two other theological virtues—faith and charity. Paul ties them together into an original triad in the earliest scriptural texts of the New Testament (1 Thess. 1:3, 5:8; 1 Cor. 13:13). Together, they become one of the first ethical claims made on the earliest Christian communities. Just as Christians were known for their faith and love, similarly they were known for their hope for the coming of the kingdom.

Moreover, the three theological virtues are complements. Thomas calls faith "the substance of things we await, the evidence of things that appear not" (II.II.4.1). He describes charity as union with God, neighbor, and self (II.II.23.3). Hope is the virtue that makes possible the journey from faith to love (II.II.17.1).

The wisdom of Paul, Augustine, Thomas, and others is to see that the virtue of faith must turn to hope and hope to charity: by knowing God, we hope in God's promises and live in God's love. As Paul, Thomas, and so many others in the tradition have taught us, faith without love is not a living faith. There are those who believe that following rules precisely and being loyal to doctrines is faith, but faith is much larger than institutions or rules in and of themselves. Faith is the virtue of one who believes in the living God of love. When the church focuses on embodying and witnessing love for its own members and the world, it is at its best.

Second, we need leaders who are models of hope. Hope supports us in faith through the journey of pursuing love as the unity of minds and hearts in God and in the kingdom. Inasmuch as hope prompts us to pursue this end, we look to those who live in hope to become our leaders. Because we need guidance for the journey and because we need to move from the shared faith to a shared love, we need to be led in hope.

Third, Christian hope is deeply realistic because it is rooted in the cross. As such, Christian hope never lets us dream of imaginary worlds: Christian hope rejects utopianism and any other pipe dream. Christian hope is, rather, the virtue for a very real journey. It allows us to see where we are and where we need to go. Through Christian hope, the prophets are able to read the signs of the times. They can see where we are because of their hope in God. Prophets always see the journey as difficult, and this again is an insight of Paul when he writes about the groans of those in hope (Rom. 8) and of Thomas Aquinas when he writes of the arduousness of hope (II.II.17.3).

I remind my students often that whenever they think of Christian hope, they should locate themselves not at some joyous endpoint, but rather in a moment of great suffering, and often I suggest that they think of funerals. At a funeral, there are some who do not believe and who therefore have no Christian hope. For them, a funeral brings closure. They consider their loved one who died and they hope to keep them alive in their hearts and memories. For believers, however, the funeral captures the ambiguity of being in an in-between time: the sense of our deep sorrow over the loss of someone with whom we hope to be reunited. For Christians there is no closure at a funeral, for we hope for a union that we do not yet have.

I press my students to consider how they would preach at the funeral of a child. How would they articulate hope to grieving parents? They often choose to be silent, but I tell them that while others are called to silence, the preacher at a funeral does not have that right. Where should they begin? I urge them to approximate the sense of loss of the grieving parents, to be where the parents are, to enter into their darkness.

Here I think on the death of my brother Bobby at twenty-six, or my niece Megan at nineteen. When my enormously resilient niece died after three years of fighting leukemia, we were all devastated, depressed, and exhausted. One of the consolations I found was in a letter that the theologian Dietrich Bonhoeffer wrote on Christmas Eve, 1943, from prison: "Nothing can make up for the absence of someone whom we love; and it would be wrong to try to find a substitute; we must simply hold out and see it through. That sounds very hard at first, but at the same time it is a great consolation, for the gap, as long as it remains unfulfilled, preserves the bonds between us. It is nonsense to say that God fills the gap; God does not fill it, but on the contrary, God keeps the gap empty and so helps us to keep alive our former communion with each other even at the cost of pain."[1] My hope is that on this arduous pilgrimage, I will always have that wanting to be reunited in love with Megan and Bobby kept alive until the end. Christian hope never fills the void but keeps it realistically empty; it testifies, in fact, to the empty tomb, the place where Christian hope was born.

Fourth, no one can speak to us about hope unless they first are our companions. Christian hope is not so much about the point of departure (our baptism in faith) nor about the point of arrival (the kingdom of God), but rather about being along the way. The hopeful leader walks with us in our journey. Moses, for instance, led the people to the Promised Land, but for forty years he was with the people of Israel in the desert.

Gandhi's credibility was also found in his ability to be with both Muslims and Hindus. Martin Luther King Jr. could only speak to us about a dream because he stood with both blacks and whites, as he eloquently tells us in his "Letter from a Birmingham Jail."[2] These are leaders who entered into the chaos that we pilgrims live day in and day out.

Of course, the same is true of Jesus Christ. In his mercy, Christ entered into the chaos of our humanity. That is why the hope that Christ brings is so deeply rooted in our history. Becoming one like us in all things but sin, Jesus Christ transforms us into a people of hope not simply because of what he promises, but because he is Emmanuel: "God who is with us." One can only be a real leader by entering into our journey and discovering exactly where we are. By knowing where we are, our leaders can imagine in hope where we actually ought to arrive.

Here I recall a gesture by Pope John XXIII. After his first papal Christmas mass, the pope left Vatican City and visited the prisoners of Regina Coeli. He arrived, explaining, "You could not come to see me so I have come to see you." The event was remarkable. It is recorded on the central bronze doors of St. Peter's today. In the middle of the left panel is John stretching his hands through prison bars, grasping the prisoners' hands while calling them his brothers.

By that simple "being with," leaders nourish their community with a sense of value and self-worth often missing in human experience. As a result, leaders help make the journey more hope-filled because some of the arduousness has been alleviated.

Fifth, since our end is to be in love, hopeful leaders labor to be reconciling. This is no easy task. We know that by watching children at play, we often see how they descend quickly into arguing and fighting. To learn to get along with others is not a childhood goal, however, but a lifelong task. Thus, when we look to the great leaders of the past, we see that inevitably the community that they led was fractious. Jesus found his disciples that way, as did King and Gandhi. In each instance, they attempted to reconcile their members.

In 2 Corinthians 5, Paul calls us to be ambassadors of reconciliation. All the more so, then, the hopeful Christian leader must be a reconciler. For a Christian to be a leader in hope, he or she must inevitably face the task of being an ambassador of reconciliation, and this, of course, is something that many recognize, but few today are doing.

It is a commonplace to say that the scandal of Christianity is in its broken communion, in its inability to become one. But the real shame of Christianity is not in its doctrinal differences but in the mean-spirited infighting within the denominations. When the Mennonite theologian Joseph Kotva and I invited twenty-five Catholic, Protestant, and Orthodox ethicists to contribute to our collection about church leadership and ethics, they almost all wanted to write about the lack of fairness and civility within, and not just among, the denominations. One ethicist after another found that even the ground rules of basic decency were abrogated when certain "doctrinal" matters were discussed.[3] When these arguments occur, do our leaders search to bring us into reconciliation, or do they actually participate in the marginalization of their own members?

Hope is made real in the leader's call to reconciliation. I heard that call in a most uncommon place. On the first Sunday after September 11, I said mass at a medium security prison for women. I asked the two hundred women there what they hoped for in light of the tragedy. One woman hoped to learn that violence begets violence, that lack of mutual respect breaks down the body politic, and that promoting dialogue is the only way to foster community. The two hundred women—all there for significant crimes they committed—stood and gave her a thunderous applause. That call to reconciliation we expect to hear from our leaders.

Sixth, hope finds expression in the hard work of leaders: we need to see our leaders laboring. Today, much of leadership focuses on speeches and promises. But real leadership is found in those persons who in hope labor to move us forward. All true leaders therefore literally lead: Moses leads the Jews through the desert, Jesus leads the twelve to Jerusalem, Martin Luther King Jr. leads the nation into civil rights legislation.

Real leadership is not marked by victory, much as that is the aim: Moses wants the Promised Land; Jesus, the kingdom; King, equality. But their leadership is expressed by them both being with us on the journey and laboring at the forefront of our common trek. They need to go before us with an energy and a commitment that expresses itself in human tiredness and sweat, which in turn evidences the hope we need to go forward.

Seventh, hope-filled leadership is rooted in asceticism. After first withdrawing to the desert for forty days, Jesus subsequently sought quiet places in order to consider his journey and the kingdom. Whenever he came out of prayer, he became more fixed on his journey, more set on Jerusalem.

In analogous ways, Martin Luther King Jr. retreated to prayer and fasting as purifying actions before he preached and led. He went from town to town knowing of plots against his life, and yet, with his faith in the Gospels and by confronting his fear in these ascetical practices, he articulated for us his dream. Gandhi likewise led a nation by first taking himself and those nearest to him into ascetical exercises so as to purge themselves of their more disagreeable natures. These ascetical practices allowed the leaders to be transformed.[4]

These ascetical practices are not escapes from the world. Through them, leaders discover that they are called not to avoid the world but to enter more deeply into it, and there they see points of light upon the horizon of our expectations. Thus, Jesus could show us, in parables, the kingdom of God, and Martin Luther King Jr. shared with us his view from the mountaintop.

In asceticism we too become a people of hope. Like my students who have discovered hope from the viewpoint of suffering, in absence we find the ground for hope. It is always somewhere near the cross or the empty tomb.

Eighth, today we lack asceticism, in part because, as we have seen, we are a presumptuous generation. This harsh description of our present condition needs comment.

I noted earlier that while former generations erred in their despair, ours is known for its presumption. In previous generations, we remember how bishops and theologians frequently referred to church members as the *massa damnata*, an incredibly despairing insight from the early medieval era all the way to the near present that maintained that most people were damned to hell. Around the 1950s we began to consider the breadth of the mercy of God and see the frequency with which the scriptures pointed to the offer of salvation as extended to all people. We began to repudiate the despairing notion of *massa damnata* and focused instead on our hope in the mercy of God.

Maybe a generation later, we moved from the universal offer of God's mercy to the universal claim of humanity's goodness. Certainly, there is a goodness in humanity, for we are in God's image, but there remains a presumptuousness about how pervasive that goodness actually is. We consider ourselves so good that we need to wonder why Christ died, why there was the cross, whether we really need God's mercy, why there is a sacrament of reconciliation.

We have come full term in an incredibly self-serving circle: from the despairing belief that the majority of persons are going to hell (a self-serving belief since invariably many who preached this believed that everyone else was damned) to the equally self-serving presumptuous belief that we all merit salvation because we are so good. Anyone who spends but a jot of time to consider the sorry state of our moral lives recognizes the pervasiveness of sin in our pettiness and jealousies, the limitedness of the human condition, and the profound need we have for the redemption and the cross of Christ.

We should believe in the universal offer of salvation, but we should never forget the parable about the wedding guest who failed to bother to put on the wedding garment (Matt. 22:11–14; also the unforgiving steward in Matt. 18:23–35). In that parable we need to know that first-century wedding guests were always presented with wedding robes to wear at the wedding celebration. The guest is ejected not because he did not bring with him appropriate garb but because he does not bother to accept the robes that would have been offered to him at his arrival. Therein we recognize his presumption and our need for God's mercy.

The reader might be surprised by this apparently bleak outlook. But presumption is particularly difficult to discern because evil is especially deceptive. The theologian Franz Böckle noted that no one knows their sinfulness until they begin to acknowledge it and then the effective act of confessing allows them to see the depth of their sinfulness. But those who do not acknowledge their sinfulness cannot know it. Therein we learn the catch-22 of presumption: the presumptuous can never know how presumptuous they really are.

We should not hesitate to recognize that in all likelihood we are probably a lot worse than we think we are. Again, some readers might find this jarring. I remember years ago, being first jarred by reading Martin Luther in a course with John O'Malley. Luther did not tire of telling his readers how bad they were. In my presumptuous years, I asked John, why did they bother to listen to Luther? "Because he spoke the truth," he responded.

Ninth, humility helps overcome presumption. Humility is not self-deprecation, but rather the virtue for knowing the place of one's power in God's world. This is the humility of Jesus before Pilate, of Mary in the Magnificat, of Paul narrating his call, and of the incredible Mary Magdalene holding on to the risen Christ in the garden. In each instance they recognize their power in God's world and they do so as an act of indebtedness to the God who gave them this power.

Humility is the virtue, therefore, that trains us in the exercise of that power. The more we practice humility, the more we understand the power that we, as leaders, are called to exercise. Unfortunately, as the recent crisis has taught us, church leadership has not done much in the study of their exercise of power.

Here I ask you to bear with me a moment as I try to make the point that, in comparison to the training of other professionals, the training for priestly, pastoral, and episcopal leadership has very little real sustained instruction on the exercise of power. In the formation of students at almost every type of professional school, their ethics courses are about the right exercise of power by the specific professional. Medical ethics is about the proper exercise of power regarding research, the care of patients, the communication of information, and the respect of confidentiality. These medical ethics courses are designed to help future physicians, nurses, and researchers to exercise properly their power in the medical field. Similarly, in law schools, students learn in their ethics courses about responsibilities to their clients, the law, the court, and the public; business ethics is about the norms that business leaders need to observe for right conduct in social and financial commerce.

When ethics is taught in the seminary or the divinity school, it is not about how to be a good priest or lay minister, or about what power priests, bishops, or pastors have and exercise; rather, it is about whether the laity engage in proper conjugal relations, about whether reproductive technologies are compatible with church teaching, whether the sanctity of life is being upheld by politicians and others responsible for the common good. We teach future clergy and ministers everything there is in ethics except the ethical responsibilities of the priest or lay minister. No other profession, except those in the academy, so abstains itself and its leaders from instruction on the ethical exercise of power.

Consider this: a seminarian in the early 1980s asked his rector whether there would be more on due process in the newly revised code of canon law. The rector responded: "We have no need for due process; we live by the law of charity." If presumption is the contemporary contrary to hope, then it shows itself most evidently by the failure to address more cogently the need we have for understanding the exercise of power by our leadership.

Tenth, one way of exercising one's power responsibly is by acknowledging one's faults. This is not easy. In our presumptuous world, few people apologize. The Japanese have not acknowledged Pearl Harbor; the United States has said nothing about Hiroshima or, worse, Nagasaki. Our pope has apologized for his predecessors' actions, but few leaders ever acknowledge their own failures.

I keep learning the importance of this lesson. I teach an introductory ethics course at Weston Jesuit. The course is very popular and I try to cover a variety of topics and perspectives. One time I entered the class to lecture on the relationship between spirituality and morality; it would be the first time in my many years of giving the course that I actually delivered a lecture on this topic. I was quite pleased with what I was about to offer. As I began, a student, who in earlier classes had expressed disagreements with me, blindsided me by asking a sarcastic question. I was so caught off guard by his remark that I responded in kind and within a minute "put him in his place." I then began my lecture on spirituality.

I could not sleep that night. During the next class I publicly acknowledged to the student that I would probably never measure up to his expectations. I then turned to the class and said, "Nonetheless, I misused my authority. I used my power to put him in his place and harmed him, myself, and the rest of you." I apologized to him and them and concluded by saying three words: "I was wrong."

We learned more in that two-minute uneasy admission that climaxed in the simple but difficult words ("I was wrong") than anything else I taught that semester. I learned that my authority in their midst grew and was not diminished by my apology.

If a person believes that an acknowledgment of personal fault will undermine her or his authority, that person has very little hope. Leaders who acknowledge their faults develop an honesty, a transparency, and a trust with their constituency and give their community grounds to hope in them. When that happens they can truly be ambassadors of reconciliation and reliable guides along the way.

Study Questions

How do you define hope?

Can you see some of your friends as particularly hope-filled? What characteristics of their lives makes you think that they are hope-filled?

What, in your mind, makes for a good leader? Give the description of a real person whom you think is a leader.

Why are apologies so difficult?

"To Live Likewise"

Catholic characters in books, plays, television shows, and movies are often caricatures of everyday Catholics. The "Catholic" character is typecast, predictably, by excessive feelings of sinfulness and guilt, and an almost neurotic need for repentance and reconciliation. We are familiar with this identification in our popular and pervasive culture, and, as with a lot of typecasting, we can recognize an element of truth in it among its many unexamined but exaggerated presuppositions.

The Catholic identity, however, is not only shaped by worries over sinfulness. We know that the Catholic community has been shaped by a long, living tradition that calls us to be free from sin and to follow Christ. From our own experience we know that the wisdom of our tradition has commanded us to love, has promoted the primacy of the conscience, and has given us a context to talk about our own suffering and to listen to the suffering of others. These lessons we have learned throughout our lives in the Catholic community, and, hopefully, on these pages in this book, we have become reacquainted yet again with the wisdom they bear.

The tradition has also provided us with a variety of texts to receive its wisdom. We have heard sermons about Jesus, catechetical instruction on the Ten Commandments, guidance on the virtues, and invitations to engage in the works of mercy.

We have been formed by these lessons and texts. They are not simply found in words on paper or heard in classrooms, however. They are expressed through a variety of practices and deeds that help to shape us into living and active disciples of Christ.

We know that it is not by wishes but by concrete actions that we become the people we want to become. Our tradition encourages us therefore not simply to listen and understand, but to act and to imitate. By following the person of Christ, we learn more and more what it means to respond to our baptismal call and become true Christians.

Consider again the parable of the Good Samaritan. In that one parable we learn who the neighbor is, that mercy constitutes love, that the call to love is a call to respond actively to the one in need, but that all these lessons are made possible first by the deeds of the merciful Christ who has been our own personal Good Samaritan. That is, Christ's actions make possible in us our healing so that we can attend to others.

Because Christ's actions have been continuous for two millennia and because the church has been that inn where we have all been brought to live, we have learned that we can only respond to our neighbor in need because we were first recognized by Christ as in need ourselves. We know within ourselves what Christ has already accomplished in us.

What Christ has accomplished in us is not something that remains in ideas or dreams or wishes. What he has won for us are timeless lessons for living and loving.

Our consciences, for instance, are not privileged places for doing whatever we want or for pursuing whatever goals we set. Our consciences are those privileged places where we are specifically and perpetually summoned by God to avoid sin, be merciful, and attend to suffering. Our consciences are where we hear the call to act as Christ has. Through our consciences we are not free to be idly whomever we wish to be; rather, through our consciences we are bound to Christ.

Among all the Gospels, it is in the oldest one, the Gospel of Mark, that we find the most evident urgency in Christ's own mission. In there we see Jesus Christ's relentless pursuit of God's will, which becomes fully accepted in Jerusalem.

We, too, are summoned to Jerusalem. Through our tradition we have learned the wisdom we need to get there. It is only by trusting in him and living likewise that we will help one another to get there.

Notes

Introduction

1. John Mahoney, *The Making of Moral Theology: A Study of the Roman Catholic Tradition* (New York: Oxford University Press, 1987).

2. Gilbert Meilaender and William Werpehowski, eds., *Oxford Handbook of Theological Ethics* (New York: Oxford University Press, forthcoming).

3. John T. McNeill and Helen M. Gamer, eds., *Medieval Handbooks of Penance* (New York: Columbia University Press, 1990).

4. Henry Lea, *The History of Auricular Confession and Indulgences in the Latin Church* (Philadelphia: Lea Brothers, 1896), 1.230.

5. Leonard Boyle, *The Setting of the* Summa Theologiae *of Saint Thomas* (Toronto: Pontifical Institute of Medieval Studies, 1982).

6. Thomas Slater, *A Manual of Moral Theology*, second edition (New York: Benziger Brothers, 1908), vol. 1, 5–6. In his "Cases of Conscience," he writes that the object of moral theology "is not to place high ideals of virtue before the people and train them in Christian perfection . . . its primary object is to teach the priest how to distinguish what is sinful from what is lawful . . . it is not intended

for edification nor for the building up of character." As quoted in Henry McAdoo, *The Structure of Caroline Moral Theology* (London: Longmans, 1949), 10–11.

7. Second Vatican Council, "Optatam Totius," in *Vatican Council II: The Conciliar and Post-Conciliar Documents*, ed. Austin Flannery (Northport, N.Y.: Costello Publishing, 1988), 720.

8. Margaret Farley, "How Shall We Love in a Postmodern World?" in *The Annual of the Society of Christian Ethics 1994*, ed. Harlan Beckley (Washington, D.C.: Georgetown University Press, 1994), 3–10.

Chapter 1

1. Josef Fuchs, *Human Values and Christian Morality* (Dublin: Gill and MacMillan, 1970).

2. Pope John Paul II, "The Splendor of the Truth," *Origins*, October 14, 1993, 297–336; Joseph Cardinal Ratzinger, *Wahrheit, Werte, Macht: Prüfsteine der pluralistischen Gesellschaft* (Freiburg: Herder, 1993).

3. James Keenan, *Commandments of Compassion* (Franklin, Wis.: Sheed & Ward, 1999).

4. Karl Rahner, *Foundations of Christian Faith: An Introduction to the Idea of Christianity* (New York: Herder and Herder, 1983).

5. Gérard Gilleman, *The Primacy of Charity in Moral Theology* (Westminster, Md.: Newman Press, 1959). See also Peter Black and James Keenan, "The Evolving Self-understanding of the Moral Theologian: 1900–2000," *Studia Moralia* 39 (2001): 291–327.

6. St. Augustine, *The Confessions of St. Augustine*, book 10, paragraph 27.

7. Edward Vacek, *Love, Human and Divine: The Heart of Christian Ethics* (Washington, D.C.: Georgetown University Press, 1994); Vacek, "Love for God—Is It Obligatory?" in *The Annual of the Society of Christian Ethics 1996* (Washington, D.C.: Georgetown University Press, 1996), 203–22; Vacek, "The Eclipse of Love for God," *America*, March 9, 1996: 13–16.

8. Margaret Farley, *Personal Commitments* (San Francisco: Harper & Row, 1986), 131–32; Farley, "New Patterns of Relationship between Women and Men: The Beginnings of a Moral Revolution," *Theological Studies* 36 (1975): 627–46; Farley, "How Shall We Love in a Postmodern World?" in *The Annual of the Society of Christian Ethics 1994* (Washington, D.C.: Georgetown University Press, 1994), 3–10.

9. Frederick Crowe, "Complacency and Concern in the Thought of St. Thomas," *Theological Studies* 20 (1959): 1–39, 198–230, 343–95.

10. Hugo Rahner, *Ignatius the Theologian* (New York: Herder and Herder, 1968).

11. Stephen Pope, *The Evolution of Altruism and the Ordering of Love* (Washington, D.C.: Georgetown University, 1994); see also his "Expressive Individualism and True Self-Love: A Thomistic Perspective," *Journal of Religion* 71, no. 3 (1991): 384–99.

CHAPTER 2

1. "In hoc quippe mundo humana anima quasi more navis est contra ictum fluminis conscendentis: uno in loco nequaquam stare permittitur, quia ad ima relabitur, nisi ad summa conetur." Gregory, Reg. Past. p. III, c. 34: ML 77, 118c.

2. "In via vitae non progredi regredi est." Bernard, Serm II in festo. Purif., n. 3: ML 183, 369 C.

3. "In via Dei stare retrocedere est." Thomas attributes the quote to Bernard in In III Sen d29,a8,qla2,1a, and to Gregory in ST II-II,24,6 ob3.

4. John Glaser, "Conscience and Superego: A Key Distinction," *Theological Studies* 32 (1971): 30–47, at 36.

5. Thomas Aquinas, Scriptum super libros Sententiarum, IV, 38. 2. 4 q.a 3; see also IV. 27. 1. 2. q.a. 4 ad3; IV. 27. 3. 3. expositio. Besides his *Commentary*, Thomas established clearly in *De veritate* (q. 17, a.4.), the Quodlibetales (III. 12. 27; VIII. 6. 13; IX. 7), his commentaries on Romans (chap. 14, lect. 2), and Galatians (5, lect. 1) and the *Summa theologiae* (I. II. q. 19, a.5) that it is always sinful to go against one's conscience.

6. James F. Keenan, "Can a Wrong Action Be Good? The Development of Theological Opinion on Erroneous Conscience," *Église et Théologie* 24 (1993): 205–21.

7. On this distinction, see James F. Keenan, "A New Distinction in Moral Theology: Being Good and Living Rightly," *Church* 5 (1989): 22–28; and Keenan, *Goodness and Rightness in Thomas Aquinas'* Summa Theologiae (Washington, D.C.: Georgetown University Press, 1992).

8. Francis Connell, *Outlines of Moral Theology* (Milwaukee: Bruce Publishing Company, 1953), 39.

9. Iris Murdoch, "Against Dryness: A Polemical Sketch," in *Revisions*, ed. Stanley Hauerwas and Alasdair MacIntyre (Notre Dame, Ind.: University of Notre Dame Press, 1983), 43–50, at 43.

CHAPTER 3

1. I should note that invariably those with poor self-esteem and other truly burdensome dispositions read this and are not helped. They

think I am suggesting that they should think worse of themselves. But I am not. It helps us to remember the old saying that virtue is the mean between extremes. Thus, courage is the mean between cowardice and foolhardiness. Similarly, we have a tendency to over- and underestimate ourselves. Those with low self-esteem underestimate themselves. My warning is for those of us (myself included) who overestimate themselves.

2. James F. Keenan, "The Problem with Thomas Aquinas's Concept of Sin," *Heythrop Journal* 35 (1994): 401–20.

3. John Mahoney, *The Making of Moral Theology* (Oxford: Clarendon Press, 1987), 32.

4. Albert Camus, *The Plague* (New York: Vintage Press, 1991).

5. David Burrell and Stanley Hauerwas, "Self-Deception and Autobiography," in *Truthfulness and Tragedy*, by Stanley Hauerwas, Richard Bondi, and David B. Burrell (Notre Dame, Ind.: University of Notre Dame Press, 1977), 82–100

6. Franz Böckle, *Fundamental Moral Theology* (New York: Pueblo Publishing, 1980).

7. I do not mean by the failure to bother to love the example of being angry with someone. That may or may not be out of love. The issue in these chapters on sin and conscience is not how we love rightly, a very big issue indeed, but rather whether we love in the first place.

8. Martin Luther King Jr., "Letter from Birmingham City Jail," in *A Testament of Hope: The Essential Writings of Martin Luther King, Jr.*, ed. James M. Washington (San Francisco: Harper and Row, 1986), 289–302; Reinhold Niebuhr, *Moral Man and Immoral Society: A Study in Ethics and Politics* (New York: Scribner, 1960).

9. On the different understandings of this parable, see Gilbert Meilaender, "Grace, Justification through Faith, and Sin," in

Ecumenical Ventures in Ethics: Protestants Engage Pope John Paul II's Moral Encyclicals, ed. Reinhard Hutter and Theodor Dieter (Grand Rapids, Mich.: Eerdmans, 1997), 60–83.

Chapter 4

1. Daniel Simundson, *Faith Under Fire* (Minneapolis: Augsburg Publishing, 1980), 144.

2. Elaine Scarry, *The Body in Pain: The Making and Unmaking of the World* (New York: Oxford University, 1985), 27–59, at 49.

3. J. David Pleins, "'Why Do You Hide Your Face?' Divine Silence and Speech in the Book of Job," *Interpretation* 48 (July 1994): 229–40, at 230.

4. Marcel Sarot, "Auschwitz, Morality and the Suffering of God," *Modern Theology* 7 (1991): 135–52.

5. Paul Nelson, "The Problem of Suffering," *The Christian Century* 108 (May 1, 1991): 491.

6. Barbara Bozak, "Suffering and the Psalms of Lament," *Église et Théologie* 23 (1992): 325–38.

7. M. Shawn Copeland, "'Wading Through Many Sorrows': Towards a Theology of Suffering in a Womanist Perspective," in *Feminist Ethics and the Catholic Moral Tradition*, eds. Charles Curran, Margaret Farley, and Richard McCormick (New York: Paulist Press, 1996), 150.

8. Copeland, "Wading," 152–53.

9. Copeland, "Wading," 156.

10. Eric Cassell, *The Nature of Suffering* (New York: Oxford University Press, 1991), 24–25.

11. Cassell, *The Nature*, 31.

12. Edward Schillebeeckx, *Christ* (New York: Seabury Press, 1980), 675.

13. Schillebeeckx, *Christ*, 677.

14. Schillebeeckx, *Christ*, 678

15. Schillebeeckx, *Christ*, 724–25.

16. Schillebeeckx, *Christ*, 728.

17. William Placher, *Narratives of a Vulnerable God* (Louisville, Ky.: Westminster, 1994), 18–19.

18. Mary Catherine Hilkert, *Speaking with Authority* (New York: Paulist Press, 2001), 126.

19. Judith M. Noone, *The Same Fate as the Poor* (Maryknoll: Orbis, 1995), 82, quoted in Hilkert, *Speaking with Authority*, 127.

20. Sheila Cassidy, *Good Friday People* (Maryknoll: Orbis, 1991), 61, quoted in Hilkert, *Speaking with Authority*, 128.

Chapter 5

1. Stanley Hauerwas, *A Community of Character* (Notre Dame, Ind.: University of Notre Dame Press, 1981).

2. We wrote a book together on scripture and ethics: Daniel Harrington and James F. Keenan, *Jesus and Virtue Ethics: Building Bridges between New Testament Studies and Moral Theology* (Chicago: Sheed & Ward, 2002).

3. Rodney Stark, *The Rise of Christianity* (Princeton, N.J.: Princeton University Press, 1996), 147.

4. Stark, *The Rise of Christianity*, 212.

CHAPTER 6

1. James Gustafson, *Theology and Christian Ethics* (Philadelphia: United Church Press, 1974), 121–45; see also Richard Gula, *Reason Informed by Faith: Foundations of Catholic Morality* (New York: Paulist Press, 1989), 165–84.

2. Francisco de Toledo, *Summa Casuum Conscientiae Sive De Instructione Sacerdotum, Libri Septem* (Constantiae: Apud Nicolaum Kalt, 1600).

3. I have developed this in "The Casuistry of Francisco de Toledo (1532–1596)," *Mercurian Collection*, ed. Thomas McCoog (St. Louis: St. Louis University Press, 2003).

4. Feliciano Cereceda, "Tolet, François," in *Dictionnaire de théologie catholique*, ed. Bernard Loth and Albert Michel (Paris: Letouzey et Ané, 1953–1972), vol. 15, 1223–25.

5. Toledo, *Summa Casuum Conscientiae*, fol. 463

6. Toledo, *Summa Casuum Conscientiae*, fol. 344.

7. Toledo, *Summa Casuum Conscientiae*, fol. 428.

8. Thomas Aquinas, *Summa Contra Gentiles* 3.122, quoted in Josef Fuchs, *Christian Morality: The Word Becomes Flesh* (Washington, D.C.: Georgetown University Press, 1987), 47.

9. Louis Vereecke, *Storia del riposo domenicale* (Rome: Alfonsianum Press, 1973).

10. Bryan Massingale, "The African American Experience and U.S. Roman Catholic Ethics: 'Strangers and Aliens No Longer'?" in *Black and Catholic: The Challenge and Gift of Black Folk: Contributions of African American Experience and World View to Catholic Theology*, ed. Jamie Phelps (Milwaukee, Wis.: Marquette University Press, 1997).

11. Brian Tierney, *The Idea of Natural Rights: Studies on Natural Rights, Natural Law, and Church Law 1150–1625* (Atlanta, Ga.: Scholars Press, 1997).

12. Tierney, *The Idea of Natural Rights*, 54.

CHAPTER 7

1. William Spohn, *Go and Do Likewise: Jesus and Ethics* (New York: Continuum Press, 1999).

2. Rodney Stark, *The Rise of Christianity* (Princeton, N.J.: Princeton University Press, 1996), 161. See also the new social solidarity that Christianity offered to those in strife: Jaroslav Pelikan, *The Excellent Empire: The Fall of Rome and the Triumph of the Church* (San Francisco: Harper and Row, 1987); John Elliott, *A Home for the Homeless: A Sociological Exegesis of 1 Peter, Its Situation and Strategy* (Philadelphia: Fortress, 1981).

3. This information is culled from a variety of sources, especially Théodore Koehler, "Miséricorde," in *Dictionnaire de spiritualité ascétique et mystique, doctrine et histoire*, ed. Marcel Viller (Paris: G. Beauchesne et ses fils, 1980), vol. 10, 1313–28; Irenée Noye, "Miséricorde (Oeuvres de)," in *Dictionnaire*, vol. 10, 1328–50; J. M. Perrin, "Mercy, Works of," in *New Catholic Encyclopedia* (Washington, D.C.: Catholic University of America Press, 1967), 676–78.

4. John O'Malley, *The First Jesuits* (Cambridge, Mass.: Harvard University Press, 1993), 167–78.

5. Sr. Helen Prejean, *Dead Man Walking: An Eyewitness Account of the Death Penalty in the United States* (New York: Vintage Press, 1994).

Chapter 8

1. Joseph de Guibert, *The Theology of the Spiritual Life* (New York: Sheed & Ward, 1953); Jean Leclercq, Francois Vandenbroucke, and Louis Bouyer, *History of Christian Spirituality* (London: Burns and Oates, 1968).

2. Bernard McGinn, "The Human Person as Image of God," in *Christian Spirituality*, ed. Jean Leclercq, Bernard McGinn, and John Meyendorff (New York: Crossroad, 1985), 312–30, at 323. While the twelfth century marks the enormous systematic development of ascetical texts, a few appear earlier, for example, Dhuoda's *Manual for My Son* (843) and Jonas of Orleans's treatise *Instruction of the Laity* (c. 828). See Jacques Fontaine, "The Practice of Christian Life: The Birth of the Laity," in *Christian Spirituality*, 453–91.

3. Caroline Walker Bynum, *Jesus as Mother: Studies in the Spirituality of the High Middle Ages* (Berkeley: University of California Press, 1982), 109.

4. Bynum, *Jesus as Mother*, 86.

5. Francois Vandenbroucke, "Lay Spirituality in the Twelfth Century," in *History of Christian Spirituality*, 243–82.

6. Bynum, *Jesus as Mother*, 106.

7. Bynum, *Jesus as Mother*, 106.

8. On Thomas's life, the finest work is James Weisheipl, *Friar Thomas d'Aquino*, second edition (Washington, D.C.: Catholic University of America Press, 1983). The best work on his writing is Jean-Pierre Torrell, *Saint Thomas Aquinas* (Washington, D.C.: Catholic University of America Press, 1996).

9. Leonard Boyle, *The Setting for the* Summa Theologiae (Toronto: Pontifical Institute of Medieval Studies, 1982).

10. The best introduction to Thomas Aquinas's very different methods remains Marie Dominique Chenu, *Toward Understanding Saint Thomas* (Chicago: Henry Regnery, 1963).

11. See Josef Pieper, *The Four Cardinal Virtues* (Notre Dame, Ind.: University of Notre Dame Press, 1966); Jean Porter, *The Recovery of Virtue* (Louisville, Ky.: Westminster, 1990).

12. For an excellent companion to reading the second part of the *Summa Theologiae*, see Stephen Pope, ed., *The Ethics of Aquinas* (Washington, D.C.: Georgetown University Press, 2002).

13. I develop this in "Proposing Cardinal Virtues," *Theological Studies* 56 (1995): 709–29.

14. Paul Ricoeur, "Love and Justice," in *Radical Pluralism and Truth: David Tracy and the Hermeneutics of Religion*, eds. Werner G. Jeanrond and Jennifer L. Rike (New York: Crossroad, 1991), 187–202, at 196.

15. Carol Gilligan, *In a Different Voice: Psychological Theory and Women's Development* (Cambridge, Mass.: Harvard University Press, 1982).

16. Stephen Pope, "Expressive Individualism and True Self-Love: A Thomistic Perspective," *Journal of Religion* 71, no. 3 (1991): 384–99; Edward Collins Vacek, *Love, Human and Divine* (Washington, D.C.: Georgetown University Press, 1994), 239–73.

17. I develop this in "Virtue and Identity," in *Creating Identity: Biographical, Moral, Religious*, eds. Hermann Häring, Maureen Junker-Kenny, and Dietmar Mieth (London: SCM Press, 2000), 69–77.

18. For example, Martha Nussbaum, "Non-Relative Virtues: An Aristotelian Approach," in *Ethical Theory: Character and Virtue*, eds. Peter A. French, Theodore E. Uehling Jr., and Howard

K. Wettstein, Midwest Studies in Philosophy, vol. 13 (Notre Dame, Ind.: University of Notre Dame Press, 1988), 32–53.

19. Lee H. Yearley, *Mencius and Aquinas: Theories of Virtue and Conceptions of Courage* (Albany: State University of New York Press, 1990).

CHAPTER 9

1. Dietrich Bonhoeffer, *Letters and Papers from Prison* (New York: Macmillan Press, 1967), 116.

2. Martin Luther King Jr., "Letter from Birmingham City Jail," *A Testament of Hope: The Essential Writings of Martin Luther King, Jr.*, ed. James M. Washington (San Francisco: Harper and Row, 1986), 289–302.

3. James F. Keenan and Joseph Kotva Jr., eds., *Practice What You Preach* (Franklin, Wis.: Sheed & Ward, 1999).

4. James MacGregor Burns, *Transforming Leadership: The Pursuit of Happiness* (New York: Atlantic Monthly Press, 2003).

Index

About the Author

James F. Keenan, SJ, is the Founders Professor of Theology at Boston College. He entered the New York Province of the Society of Jesus in 1970 and was ordained a priest in 1982. He graduated with a bachelor's degree in English and philosophy from Fordham University (1976) and a master's of divinity from Weston Jesuit School of Theology (1982). He studied moral theology at the Gregorian University in Rome with Fathers Josef Fuchs and Klaus Demmer and received a licentiate (1984) and a doctorate (1988).

He taught at Fordham University from 1987 to 1991 and at Weston Jesuit School of Theology from 1991 to 2005. He has recently been appointed to Boston College. He was Consultant to the National Catholic Conference of Bishops for the Revision of the *Ethical and Religious Directives for Catholic Health Care Institutions* (1988–1995) and a group leader of the United States' Surgeon General's Task Force on Responsible Sexual Conduct (2000–2002). He has been on the editorial board of *Theological Studies* since 1991 and the board of directors of the Society of Christian Ethics (2001–2005). He is the editor of two book series: *Moral Traditions*, at Georgetown University Press, and the *Boston College Church 21* series at Crossroads/Herder and Herder.

Toward a Global Vision of Catholic Moral Theology: Reflections on the Twentieth Century and *The Works of Mercy: The Heart of Catholicism* are his newest books. His earlier works include *Goodness and Rightness in Thomas Aquinas's* Summa Theologiae, *Virtues for Ordinary Christians, Commandments of Compassion, Jesus and Virtue Ethics* (with Dan Harrington), and *Moral Wisdom: Lessons and Texts from the Catholic Tradition* (first edition). He has a book coming out in the fall: *A History of Catholic Moral Theology in the Twentieth Century: From Confessing Sins to Liberating Consciences.* He is now writing two books: one on the *Ethics of the Word* and one with Daniel Harrington on Paul and virtue ethics.

He edited *Practice What You Preach: Virtues, Ethics and Power in the Lives of Pastoral Ministers and Their Congregations* (2000), which won the Catholic Press Award for best work in pastoral theology, and *Catholic Ethicists on HIV/AIDS Prevention*, which won the best work in ethics from the Jesuit Honor Society, Alpha Sigma Nu (2003). With Jean Bartunek and Mary Ann Hinsdale, Father Keenan edited *Church Ethics and Its Organizational Context: Learning from the Sex Abuse Scandal in the Catholic Church* (2005).

He is the chair of the international committee Catholic Theological Ethics in the World Church, and helped host the First International Cross-cultural Conference for Catholic Theological Ethicists in July 2006 in Padua, Italy. He subsequently edited *Catholic Theological Ethics in the World Church: The Plenary Papers from the First Cross-cultural Conference on Catholic Theological Ethics* (2007), which has appeared with publishing houses in New York, Buenos Aires, Bologna, Bangalore, and Manila, and is expected to come out shortly from Brazil as well.

He has published over three hundred essays, articles, and reviews in over twenty-five international journals. He has been a fellow at the Institute of Advanced Studies at the University of Edinburgh (1994), the Center of Theological Inquiry, Princeton (1995, 1996), and the Instituto Trentino di Cultura (2007, 2008). He has been adjunct professor at the Gregorian University in Rome (2000, 2002), Loyola School of Theology in Manila (2001, 2003), and Dharmaram Vidya Kshetram in Bangalore (2007). He held the Tuohy Chair at John Carroll University, Cleveland (1999), and the Gasson Chair at Boston College (2003–2005).

He is planning for the next conference of theological ethicists, "In the Currents of History: From Trento to the Future," to be held July 24–27, 2010, in Trent, Italy.